THE CALL OF THE MILD

TORRY MARTIN & DOUG PETERSON

HARVEST HOUSE PUBLISHERS
EUGENE, OREGON

Cover design by Kyler Dougherty

Cover Images © Rorshak / www.rorshak.com (Lion provided by Cumberland University, Lebanon, Tennessee); Artemisia1508 / iStockphoto

Chapter 30 includes partial lyrics from
Danger Zone (from *Top Gun*)
Words and Music by Giorgio Moroder and Tom Whitlock.
Copyright © 1986 Sony/ATV Music Publishing LLC and Budde Music, Inc.
All Rights on behalf of Sony/ATV Music Publishing LLC administered by Sony/ATV Music Publishing LLC, 424 Church Street, Suite 1200, Nashville, TN 37219.
All rights on behalf of Budde Music, Inc. administered by WB Music Corp.
International copyright secured. All rights reserved.
Reprinted by permission of Hal Leonard LLC and Alfred Music.

The stories you are about to read are true...for the most part. Some names, places, and details have been changed in an effort to prolong my life.

THE CALL OF THE MILD
Copyright © 2018 by Torry Martin and Doug Peterson
Published by Harvest House Publishers
Eugene, Oregon 97408
www.harvesthousepublishers.com

ISBN 978-0-7369-7159-1 (pbk.)
ISBN 978-0-7369-7160-7 (eBook)

Library of Congress Cataloging-in-Publication Data

Names: Martin, Torry, 1961- author.
Title: Call of the mild : misadventures in Africa, Hollywood, and other wild places/
    Torry Martin and Doug Peterson.
Description: Eugene, Oregon : Harvest House Publishers, 2018.
Identifiers: LCCN 2017046131 (print) | LCCN 2018001539 (ebook) | ISBN
    9780736971607 (ebook) | ISBN 9780736971591 (pbk.)
Subjects: LCSH: Martin, Torry, 1961- | Christian biography—Alaska—Biography.
Classification: LCC BR1725.M264 (ebook) | LCC BR1725.M264 A3 2018 (print) |
    DDC 277.3/083092 [B]—dc23
LC record available at https://lccn.loc.gov/2017046131

Printed in the United States of America

18 19 20 21 22 23 24 25 26 / VP-GL / 10 9 8 7 6 5 4 3 2 1

From Torry
To my amazing parents, Billy and Verna Martin
For all that you've done for me, you should have 100 books dedicated
to you, and at least 99 of them should be manuals on how to raise a
difficult child. The other one should be How to Work with What
You've Got. *I love you both.*

And to my best friend, Robert Browning
I know I dedicated the last book to you, but... "Whatever."

From Doug
To Scott Irwin
I am speechless. I am without speech. Thank you for being a wise and
wonderful friend. In the immortal words of Kramer, "Yo-Yo Ma."

ACKNOWLEDGMENTS

First of all, I need to acknowledge that I nearly drove Rob crazy while writing this book. So thank you, Rob, for everything you do. Without you, this book would not exist. You are my biggest blessing.

In addition, I'd like to thank Marshal Younger. We met 18 years ago when we were both writers for *Adventures in Odyssey*, and since then we've gone on to write 11 screenplays together. Marshal has become a second best friend. His invaluable help transformed this book, and Doug and I are indebted to him in ways that words cannot convey.

The third person in my Torry trinity of best buddies is Jack Aiken. I would like to thank Jack and his lovely wife, Ann, for their faithful friendship and for the guidance they have given to me over the years.

In addition, I thank the incredibly talented Rory White, who did the cover and back cover photography for this book, as well as for *Of Moose and Men*. I look forward to working together with him for many years to come. Also, thanks to Lucas Wilson for photographing my return to Alaska, and to Don Catlett at Clearly See Media for his tremendous help with the pictures for this book.

Also, thanks to Terry Glaspey and Gene Skinner at Harvest House Publishers for not lopping off my head when I asked for my fourth deadline extension. You believed in this project from the beginning, and I appreciate all that you did in making the book a reality, except for giving me a word-count limit. (Word counts apply to acknowledgments too, or I would've made this longer.)

I take full credit for any lapses in grammar. Terry, Gene, Marshal, and Doug all allowed me to put the book in my own voice, even at the expense of grammatical accuracy. Any grammar deficiencies are not a reflection on any of them.

Finally, I would like to acknowledge *The Chicago Manual of Style* and how *very* much I despise you. Every time I tried to use "like" as in "like I'm stupid," you would change "like" to "as if."

Like I even care.

As if!

Torry Martin

CONTENTS

FOREWORD
BY TOSCA LEE

The first time Torry Martin and I met, we were both on staff at a conference on the campus of Villanova University. We sat down at an outdoor table and talked for hours like old friends, delving into matters of God and faith as we made our way through a small vat of coffee. We also talked about writing, living with OCD, and how he'd almost wrecked a washing machine while cleaning shotgun shells for the Christmas lights he was making to accompany his moose-dropping garlands (which *definitely* don't go in the washer).

Technically, that was the second time we met. I don't remember the first, but it happened at a trade show where he lined up for a copy of my latest novel. Torry was exercising his secret superpower of encouraging and supporting the work of others who may not even know him yet. He was doing what he does best: investing in lives with the gift of his time (while nabbing a free novel of exceptional quality, of course). It's something he regularly does, tithing time to the growth of others who may not be aware that he's working on their behalf, doing good behind their backs.

Today, Torry is the kind of friend I shriek happily upon seeing and then say loudly, "Oh my gosh, is that Torry Martin? I've seen his movies!" (This probably embarrasses him, but how many friends have *you* seen on the Hallmark Channel?) Then we hug before diving into discussion as deeply as time allows—preferably over a sandwich and with a few goofy selfies.

Torry is the kind of person you can be your serious and nerdy self with. He's someone with whom you can discuss spiritual matters and the (equally crucial) best way to organize a silverware drawer and the pivotal Tupperware bin, which he and I may or may not have discussed with an exchange of photographic evidence on more than one occasion.

As a creative, Torry is a prolific mind with more ideas than he'll ever have time to produce, write, or act—each of them as funny as they are deep. A true gift to a world longing for both meaning and much-needed levity.

Most of all, he's a friend with a gift for making others feel seen and full of the potential they may not recognize in themselves. A man full of adventure with a heart for each being he finds in his path, fueled by his keen desire for God.

Each of these qualities shines through in *The Call of the Mild*—every chapter a glimpse into the man himself: hilarious, heartwarming, and wise. I pray these stories lift your spirits and encourage you as they have me.

If you've never met, heard, or read him before, I am so honored to introduce my friend Torry Martin.

Tosca Lee
New York Times bestselling author

1
HOODIEWINKED

KNOCK! KNOCK! KNOCK!

The police officer tapped on my window.

"I noticed you swerving," he said. "Could you please step out of the car, sir?"

"Okay," I replied, "but that could be a little tricky."

I tried to act as natural as possible. But as I opened my door and put my left foot out of the car, the upside-down hoodie sweatshirt I was wearing as a pair of pants started to slip down. I was holding it up with one hand, but as I stood, I felt the zipper in back starting to pull apart.

I was afraid the hoodie would fall to my feet and I would be left standing in front of McDonald's in my SpongeBob boxer shorts with a Japanese family of three watching from inside the restaurant—a bizarre dinner theater show to accompany their Big Macs.

That was when I decided to act on the weirdest thought I ever had. *I should tap dance!*

. . . .

It all started two days earlier when my dogs went missing. We have three dogs—Bear, Willow, and our newest miracle dog, Samantha. I must confess that I tend to obsess over my dogs more than the average person. That's largely due to the fact that my best friend, Rob, and I are two single Christian men sharing a house, and these dogs are our only source of physical affection. It's either hug the dogs, hug each other, or hug my poster of Gal Gadot. His beard is scratchy, and she'd give me a paper cut, so I choose the dogs.

Rob and I live in rural Tennessee, surrounded by fields and forests—plenty of space for dogs to get lost. So when Samantha and Willow went missing, Rob and I spent the next two days in our cars driving up and down country roads, calling out for them. Looking for them was exhausting, especially with so little sleep. My overactive imagination kept me awake as I feared the worst. *What if they've been stolen? What if the two dogs were separated? What if they never bring the McRib back? What if they make McRibs out of dogs?*

As if there wasn't already enough stress in my life, I had to leave that day to attend a media conference. I planned to leave at noon, but it was now four in the afternoon, and I was so busy searching for my dogs that I hadn't even packed my car for the trip yet.

I reluctantly concluded that I couldn't put off my trip any longer. So I returned home, quickly packed my car, and began a worry-filled drive at five o'clock, the time I had originally hoped to arrive at the conference.

I was only 20 miles away from home when the exclamation mark on my dashboard suddenly lit up. Either it was just as surprised as I was to be leaving so late, or it could be something else. *But what? I suppose I could dig out the manual to see what it means, but who needs a manual when you have a Rob?*

"It means your tire pressure is low," Rob explained when I phoned him. "Where'd you get your tires?"

"Sam's Club. They're under warranty."

"Where are you now?"

"I'm just nearing the exit for Sam's Club."

"Well, take that exit, go to Sam's Club, and get your tires fixed. They'll do it for free if they're under warranty."

See what I mean? The guy is brilliant.

After I waited an hour and a half at Sam's Club, they discovered a screw embedded in the tire, so they patched it up and gave me my car back. I quickly called Rob again to tell him the car was fixed, but I was now six and a half hours behind schedule. Rob, however, being Rob, had a solution.

"There's another road you can take—Celina Highway. It'll take you 40 minutes out of your way, but it'll save you an hour and a half in the long run."

I drove to a nearby Pilot station and pulled up to the middle of three gas pumps, just behind another car. While my car was fueling, I decided to dash inside to get a cup of coffee—and two large Red Bulls in case the coffee didn't work.

Then I climbed back into my car and discovered an immediate problem: two cup holders, three drinks. I have an extreme case of obsessive compulsive disorder, and my OCD mind noted that the Red Bulls matched each other, so they got the cup holders and the coffee went between my legs.

There was still a vehicle in front of me, so, already energized by a few swigs of coffee and impatient because of the time, I hurriedly put the car in reverse and prepared to go around him. But that was much easier said than done. I couldn't see out my back window, which was blocked by my five-piece luggage set with four boxes of books perilously perched on top.

I would've put some of this stuff in my trunk, but there wasn't enough room. It was already packed full with enough supplies to survive any potential crisis, including the apocalypse, whenever it comes—pre, mid, or post. I've got 'em all covered. My trunk carried my first-aid kit, winter weather safety kit, emergency bathroom supplies, a box of MREs (meals ready to eat—and I'm always ready to eat), an ice chest, and a collapsible director's chair with matching sun umbrella, just in case my car breaks down and I have to sit on the side of the road. (I have very fair skin and don't tan. I turn either a bright red or a light pink, neither of which goes with my wardrobe. Pale white goes with everything.)

I'm probably leaving something out, but I'm afraid to open my trunk to take an inventory. That would require a four-person search party, high-powered floodlights, and one of those underwater robot cameras like they used in *Titanic*.

Basically, I'm an overweight, overworrying, overpacker. I told you, it's an extreme case of OCD. Weren't you listening? Yeesh.

Anyway, I was blinded by the—wait! I also have an extreme case of ADHD. I meant to tell you earlier but got distracted. Starting again...

Blinded by the piles of luggage in the backseat, I was going to have to back up by faith. It was my Honda trust fall.

Unaware that another car had pulled up to the pump behind me, I started to back up...

HONK! HONK!

I slammed on my brakes, and the coffee went flying, immediately giving me coffee crotch. But there was no way I could change out of my now soaked shorts because my clothes were in the very bottom suitcase of my Leaning Tower of Luggage. *My next car is definitely going to have one of those fancy backup cameras.*

Frustrated but not defeated, I decided I wasn't going to allow myself to be delayed one second longer, so I got back on the road with soggy shorts and a sagging spirit. My damp shorts didn't bother me at first, but ten miles later I began to experience the first stages of driver's chafe. My plan was to pull over and change clothes once I got on Celina Highway, but you can imagine my surprise when I finally reached the road to find it completely closed down.

That's when my two GPS systems started bickering. I have a terrible sense of direction, so I always have a backup. Second opinions are always nice. The GPS on my phone had a woman's voice, the GPS in the car had a man's voice, and they couldn't agree on anything.

"In 500 feet, turn right on Madison Road," said Mrs. GPS.

"In 1,000 feet, turn left on Juniper Street," said Mr. GPS.

"Turn right on Madison Road," insisted Mrs. GPS.

"Madison Road is a school zone," Mr. GPS pointed out. "Take Juniper."

"He doesn't know what he's talking about. Take Madison!" she said.

"She always does this. She never listens to me! Take Juniper!" he said.

"Maybe I would listen to you if you showed me the courtesy of taking out the trash when I ask you to!"

"Trash day is Thursday! Why would I take it out today?"

"Today *is* Thursday!"

Pause. "Route recalculation."

Frustrated by my feuding GPS systems, I pulled to the side of the road to call Rob. "Follow the signs to Birdstown," he said.

Sitting there, still suffering from driver's chafe, I had an idea. I slipped off my gym shorts in the front seat—no easy trick for a big man. Then, contorting my body, I reached way back behind me, pushed a couple of boxes aside, lowered the backseat window, and carefully draped my shorts over it. Then I powered the window back up and wedged the shorts securely in place, giving new meaning to the word "wedgie." I made sure about three inches remained inside the car to secure them, and I left the rest of the soggy shorts outside to flap in the breeze so they could get good and dry. I was pretty impressed that I could do all of this in the cramped confines of my car. I felt like Houdini in a Honda.

I spotted the sign for Birdstown and started to follow it to the left. But 20 minutes later it started sprinkling. Realizing that I needed to get my shorts back in before they got drenched, I quickly pulled over, reached for the back window, and saw that my shorts had disappeared!

Completely vanished. And here I thought *I* was Houdini. No time to send out a search and rescue team for my shorts. I was already running late.

Then my phone rang. It was Rob, calling to check on my progress. I told him I was near Birdstown.

"I just wanted to warn you about the police," he said. "They're everywhere on those country roads, so use your cruise control."

Now I had a new worry: getting stopped for speeding by the police. If there really were cops around, I didn't want to be caught with my pants down—or off, for that matter.

The only other piece of clothing I had handy was my black hoodie on the passenger seat. This inspired a brilliant idea. I realized that if I flipped the hoodie sweatshirt upside down with the zipper facing backward and put my legs through the sleeves, I could wear it as a pair of pants. Sitting in the car, I'd look just like I was wearing black sweats.

I took off my shoes, slipped my legs through the armholes, put my shoes back on, placed my feet on the gas and brake pedals, and voila! Turns out *I'm* the genius. Who needs Rob? The sweatshirt's hood dangled between my feet, but that was a minor problem. I figured I could use it as a crumb catcher when I stopped for donuts.

So with complete confidence, off I drove in my hoodie pants, following the directions from Mr. GPS. I turned off Mrs. GPS because I already had enough voices in my head. I could squeeze in one more voice, but definitely not two. Besides, it was distracting.

"In three-quarters of a mile, turn right on Happy Valley Road," said Mr. GPS.

Happy Valley? That's gotta be a good sign. I turned right, set the cruise control, and took my foot off the pedal, relaxing it. It was now dark as I comfortably cruised down the road. Unfortunately, I'd only gone a few miles when I spied a sign indicating that the speed limit was reduced from 65 to 55. I tried to tap my brakes to disengage the cruise control, but while my foot had been relaxing, somehow it had become caught in the hood of my upside-down sweatshirt, and now

I couldn't shake it loose. As I struggled to free my foot, I saw that the speed limit was reduced again to 45, but I was still racing along at 65 miles per hour, unable to slow down!

"OH! EEK! AAAAH!"

When translated from scream-speak, this means, "My foot's stuck! HELLLLP!"

In my panic, I didn't think to push the button that turns off the cruise control. Instead, with my right hand, I reached down and tried to free my foot, giving my left hand full control of the steering wheel, which pulled the car hard left. I brought my right hand up and yanked the steering wheel hard right in a desperate struggle to bring the vehicle under control. *This isn't Happy Valley. It's Death Valley!*

"Lord, help!"

Once again, I tried to shake my foot loose, and once again I swerved...

Sirens! Flashing red lights!

I wanted to slow down, but I was unable to extract my foot from the hoodie and continued whizzing along at 65 miles per hour. I was inadvertently involved in a high-speed chase! *The police will just have to keep up. Maybe they can pull alongside me and pass the speeding ticket through the window.* I went a full mile before I finally got my foot free and was able to tap my brakes to slow down.

There was no place to pull over until I sensed a McDonald's in the distance. I can smell their fries from 20 miles away and their apple pies from 30.

After pulling into McDonald's with the police car right behind, I parked across three empty spaces. I knew the officers wouldn't be happy with me, but I wasn't happy either. The only thing happy here was...

Hmm...a Happy Meal sounds good, and we're already here anyway. I wonder if they'll give me time to—

KNOCK! KNOCK! KNOCK!

The police officer tapped on my window.

While the officer checked my proof of insurance and registration and ran my driver's license, I sat in my car and prayed an ADHD-enhanced, anxiety-ridden, Red-Bull-influenced prayer of panic. *Father, please don't let me get a ticket. Just bring my dogs home. I don't want to go to jail. Unless I can bring my dogs to jail. Maybe they can join the police academy. I hear they take dogs. I want my dogs!*

"What seems to be the problem?" the officer asked, interrupting my thoughts.

"My dogs are missing!" I blurted out without thinking.

"Sooo, that's why you were swerving? You were looking for your dogs?"

"No," I quickly said. "I was swerving 'cuz my foot caught on the hoodie and my shorts blew out."

Those words made complete sense to me but obviously not to the policeman.

"Have you been drinking, sir?"

"Yes!" I responded. "I had two 18-ounce Red Bulls. They're the big ones."

"Anything else?"

"A cup of coffee, black, no creamer. I'm a diabetic. But I only had a couple sips." (My OCD makes me provide excruciatingly painful details.)

"Could you please step out of the car, sir?"

"Okay," I said, "but that could be a little tricky."

And it turns out I was right. I still didn't want to reveal that I was wearing hoodie pants, so I tried to step out while acting as natural as possible. But as I put my left foot on the ground, the hoodie started to slip down.

I grabbed the front with my right hand to keep it from slipping further, but as I stood, I felt the zipper in back start to pull apart. So I used my left hand to keep the zipper from separating further. I looked like I was riding an imaginary horse, and I felt ridiculous, but getting booked in my SpongeBob boxers would be worse.

There were two officers. I didn't catch their names, so I'll just call them Starsky and Hutch.

"Step forward," said Officer Starsky, taking me aside to perform the first of a three-step DUI test.

"Follow my finger," he added as he slowly moved it side to side.

"You can move your finger faster," I said. "The Red Bulls kicked in, and right now I could follow a hyperactive hummingbird."

Noticing my dilated pupils, he moved on to the next step. "Now stand on one leg for as long as you can."

"O...kay."

That's when I realized that hoodies aren't designed to be worn as pants. There just isn't enough fabric between the legs/sleeves to raise one's foot properly. I tried my hardest to raise one foot, but I started to wobble and stumble. I immediately put my foot back down to regain my balance.

Officer Hutch looked at me suspiciously. I could tell he thought I was drunk. "Do you mind if we search your car?"

"Sure, go ahead," I said, giving my consent. "Let me know if you find some sunglasses. I was looking for them earlier." I gave the officer a smile. He didn't smile back. *Well, at least I know HE's sober.*

Meanwhile, my audience was growing. In addition to the Japanese family inside the McDonald's, two more people had now gathered outside to watch the show.

"Okay, sir, can you please walk a straight line, placing one foot directly in front of the other?" Officer Starsky said.

It sounded easy enough, but the hood kept tripping me, so I reached down to lift it up. But that released my grip on the "waistband," and my upside-down hoodie crashed down to my ankles like the Sweatshirt of Jericho. Realizing I was now fully exposed in my boxers, I fully committed to it. I kicked my shoes off, pulled the hoodie off my feet, and threw it triumphantly to the ground.

"Your SpongeBob's not very absorbent," Officer Starsky said.

I looked down at my boxers in horror. "It's coffee!" I explained to the officers. Then I turned to the McDonald's audience. "IT'S COF-FEE!" I shouted.

That's when I thought, *This is humiliating. The sooner I can get them to believe I'm sober, the sooner I can get this over with. Wait...I should tap dance.* In my Red Bull–influenced brain, a perfectly executed time step would immediately show them how sober I was.

Hop, step, fa-lap, ball, change! Hop, step, fa-lap, ball, change! And hold!

I'm pretty sure doing a tap dance was not part of the Kentucky field sobriety test, but it should be.

"Could a drunk do that?" I said. "Or how about this?"

If I can't convince them I'm sober, I can at least convince them I'm a Christian. Maybe one of them is a brother and will let me off the hook. I then launched into a Jesus cheer that involved some pretty compli-cated hand motions.

"Jesus is number one! He's big and He's bold and He'll save your soul! UMPH!"

The cheer ended with me standing on one leg, the other leg in the air, and my right arm in the power position. The audience at McDon-ald's broke into spontaneous applause.

"Thank you!" I said, acknowledging the crowd. I turned back to Officer Starsky, eagerly awaiting his approval.

Officer Starsky studied my face. "I think we're going to need to do the Breathalyzer."

"Yes, please!" I said enthusiastically, knowing it was the one test I would definitely pass.

As I exhaled into the device, I noticed that my audience had expanded to seven, which is God's number, making them holy wit-nesses. The officer studied the Breathalyzer and turned toward the crowd as if they were game show contestants. "What do you think?" he asked them.

"Sober!" the first person shouted.

"Sober!" the second person shouted.

Pause... "Stupid!" the third person shouted.

"Yes!" I yelled. "That's our winner!"

The officers nodded. Contestant number three was correct.

The officers had searched my car, and as they moved to put my luggage back in, I stopped them. "Wait! I've got clothes in that one, and I'd kinda like to put something on."

"We'd kinda like that too," Officer Hutch said with a chuckle. Clearly they were warming up to me—so much so that the officers opened both doors on the driver's side of the car, creating a little changing stall for me. Hutch also shielded me with his body, standing with his back to me and giving me the privacy to dig through my luggage and change my clothes.

I unzipped the piece of luggage, and as I scanned the contents, my OCD immediately kicked in. Feeling uncertain, I pulled out a pair of shorts and a pair of pants, and while holding them up, I turned to Officer Hutch. "Which do you think?"

The policeman looked at the shorts and at the pants before responding. "Well...the shorts are more casual with the shirt you're wearing."

"Yeah, but they're the wrong color," I said, noting that the shorts were brown. "Brown never goes with black."

"Maybe change the shirt?"

"Yes!" I exclaimed, reaching down and grabbing my coordinated brown-checkered shirt. As I did, I noticed the fresh, dry, clean underwear. I pulled a pair of fresh boxers out. "Would you guys mind if I—"

"NO!" Hutch said.

"Sir?" added Starsky.

"Sorry," I responded meekly. I guess even the law had its limits.

Believe it or not, this was only the beginning of what was to become the strangest seven days of my life—and for those who know me, that's saying a *lot*.

. . . .

The Call of the Mild focuses on our calling from God and the lessons I've learned as I've tried to follow mine. The lesson I learned from this experience (other than "hoodies don't make good pants" and "don't back up with coffee in your lap") is that following God's call often involves sacrifice. That may sound like a no-brainer, which happens to be my specialty, but talking about sacrifice and putting it into practice are two entirely different things.

Leaving home for seven days when my dogs were missing was one of the hardest things I've ever done. But I had made a commitment to my calling—and to the people at the conference where I was headed. By sacrificing my desire to keep searching for my dogs, I was being obedient to God, trusting that He would protect my pets while the search continued in Rob's competent hands.

Besides, in Matthew 10:37, Jesus says that anyone who loves their father, mother, son, or daughter more than Him is not worthy of Him. I was pretty sure that applied to lost dogs too.

I'll eventually come back to finish the story of this crazy week, in which so much of what I learned about my calling miraculously came together. But the rest of this story will only make sense to you if you can make sense of me. And to do that, we need to go back to the beginning.

The earth was formed from cooling magma...

Okay, too far back. Let's just go back to high school. Follow me. I'll be the one wearing the dunce cap.

2
BOOM-BOOM!

It was spaghetti Wednesday at my high school, which was always the best day of the week. But it was about to become one of the worst days of my life.

Although I loved food, I hated lunch hour in high school because I inevitably ate alone. I was the fat kid who liked theater. Even the nerds didn't want to sit with me.

As the cafeteria lady handed me my plate of spaghetti, I thought I heard my name being mentioned at the cool kids' table, followed by giggling. *At least they know my name*, I thought, trying to comfort myself.

One of the guys at the cool kids' table had been my greatest tormenter since junior high—a boy whom I'll just refer to as Biff Stanky. He was the stereotypical golden boy—good looking, popular...and a bully. I'm leaving out his real name because I'm a bit afraid he'll track me down. I haven't had my head dunked in a toilet since the twelfth grade. Well, except for that time I had to retrieve my iPhone 4, but the point is, I feel no urge to relive the experience.

Biff Stanky didn't just haunt my life at school. His bullying sometimes touched closer to home because the Stankys were our neighbors. But they were the type of neighbors you didn't want. On the outskirts of Silverdale, Washington, we lived on opposite ends of the same road, a good mile away from each other, but even that was too close for comfort. Biff lived at the top of the hill, and I lived at the bottom—a direct reflection of our positions in high school.

What's more, my dad and Mr. Stanky had a simmering conflict of their own. "Slow down!" Mr. Stanky would yell every time my father drove past their house.

"Mow your lawn!" my dad would yell back. Then he would mutter to himself, "I don't even know how he can see me over all that grass." Our families were like the Hatfields and McCoys of the Pacific Northwest.

With lunch tray in hand, I headed toward my usual table on the opposite side of the cafeteria, as far away from the cool kids as I could get. I was pleased that I wasn't hearing my theme song, a parody of a song from the musical *Grease* that went, "Look at me, I'm Sandra Dee, lousy with virginity. Won't go to bed till I'm legally wed. I can't! I'm Sandra Dee."

Biff knew my middle name was "De," so he changed the lyrics to "Look at me, I'm Torry De, lousy with obesity. Won't go to bed until I'm fully fed. I can't! I'm Torry De!" It actually would've been kind of clever if it hadn't been so demoralizing.

But as I said, I wasn't hearing the song today. *They must be giving me the day off.* But then I heard another sound coming from the cool kids' table.

"BOOM, BOOM, BOOM, BOOM!"

Steadily, other kids around the cafeteria picked up the chant: "BOOM, BOOM, BOOM, BOOM!"

It dawned on me. They were timing the BOOM-BOOM sound to match my footsteps.

"BOOM, BOOM, BOOM, BOOM!"

Eager to make it stop, I picked up my pace. But that only made it more comical, because now it sounded like a rapid-fire machine gun.

"BOOM-BOOM-BOOM-BOOM-BOOM-BOOM-BOOM-BOOM!"

Relieved to reach my table, I sat down and avoided eye contact with anyone. As I stared at my plate of spaghetti, I realized I had a problem. *I forgot my silverware!*

I gazed across the cafeteria. *There's no way I'm going back.* So I opted to eat my spaghetti with my fingers instead.

"Look!" Biff shouted. "He doesn't even use a fork! He just shovels it in!"

"Loof gree a moone!" I said. Which in full-mouth-speak means, "Leave me alone!"

Just when I thought my day couldn't get worse, I realized my very next class was gym—the only thing I dreaded more than casserole Tuesday. I wiped my hands on my shirt (I forgot my napkins too) and headed to the next torture session.

Today we were doing gymnastics, and our task was to jump on a springboard and vault over a leather pommel horse. My PE teacher was also my science teacher, and he, of all people, should be able to figure out that the physics alone would make this task impossible for me.

There I was, watching the others successfully complete this maneuver while making mental notes for my turn. Each kid sprinted down the gym floor, leaped on the springboard, and soared over the pommel horse. Then that boy would stand beside the horse and become the spotter for the next person, ready to catch him if he fell.

I hope I have a strong spotter. That's when I looked at the person standing next to me, and I realized who my spotter was going to be.

Oh no. Not Biff, I thought. *Please, NOT BIFF!*

One by one, the kids took their turns until the line finally reached Biff, the golden boy. He sprinted like a golden gazelle across the gym, hit the springboard, soared over the pommel horse, and landed victoriously with his hands raised in the air as if he had just won an Olympic medal.

He moved to the spotter position and gave me a devious smile.

Please, don't let Biff say, "Boom, boom"...Please don't let him say, "*Boom, boom.*" I wasn't a Christian at the time, so this wasn't a prayer to anyone in particular. I was just pleading with whatever force was out there in the universe.

A bead of sweat slid down my forehead. I looked around at the other kids and could see some of them grinning in anticipation. Finally, I sucked in a deep breath and took off running.

That's when it began.

"BOOM, BOOM, BOOM, BOOM!"

Biff led the chant, and the other guys joined in as I picked up my speed in an effort to get this over with.

"BOOM, BOOM, BOOM, BOOM!"

Make it stop! Just make it stop!

I leaped onto the springboard with full force and...

CRACK!

The board split in two. I hit the side of the pommel horse with my knees, lost all control, and flipped over it sideways. I landed directly on top of Biff the Golden Boy and heard another...

CRACK!

I had broken Biff's leg.

I'm sure some of you might be thinking it was great that Biff got his comeuppance. But the accident only made me an even bigger social outcast because I had broken the leg of one of our star football players.

I did eventually get revenge on my classmates, however. At our twentieth reunion, I was the only person who had the same figure *now* that I had *then* (which isn't saying much, but at least I'm consistent).

* * * * * * * * *

Whoever coined the saying "Sticks and stones may break my bones, but words will never hurt me" was wrong, and I still carry the "word scars" to prove it—with new wounds on top. Bullies never seem to outgrow the name-calling phase. They just get better at it, honing their craft like a well-skilled artist.

Recently a movie that I cowrote and starred in called *Heaven Bound* was reviewed by an atheist website that did podcasts mocking Christian films. Surprisingly, these guys seemed to like the movie, or at least found it tolerable. They even said I was funny. But then the knives came out, and they were all thrown in my direction. Of course, big guys make easy targets, so none of their knives missed. I listened as they described me as an "Irish sumo wrestler," a "walking Christmas tree," and the "Lucky Charms mascot with gout."

They started cleverly enough but went downhill fast. For the next 12 minutes, they ripped into every single aspect of my appearance, and I felt like I was in high school all over again. "What a Fatty Fat Fat," one guy said. (He must have been a fifth grader.) These criticisms were not funny or even remotely creative and were designed only to berate and belittle me. And again, for *12 minutes*! The reviewers ended with the grand finale: "Take every stereotype of an ugly person *ever*, and roll them into one, and you get this guy."

That's the one that hurt.

I tried not to let them get under my skin. My pants were already too tight. But I listened to that vicious podcast four times. Why would I do that? Probably because these guys were just saying out loud everything I already thought about myself. For me, it was confirmation. I can be my own biggest bully, and their words ran through my mind over and over again like an endless loop.

Rob was at the Anchorage airport heading home when he spotted my Facebook post about the podcast. He called me up right then and there, even though it was two a.m. my time.

"I saw your post and thought I'd call and give you some encouragement," Rob said.

"Oh!" I was caught off guard. "Well...thanks."

"Yeah, toughen up," he added. "This can't be the first time you were called ugly."

"Pardon?"

"Uh...that didn't come out right. I meant to say 'fat,' not 'ugly.' No! I mean 'stupid.'"

"Not. Helping." (This is exactly why I call Rob the Wrong Words Wonder.)

I knew he was trying to say that I must have dealt with being called names before. He just didn't need to give such specific examples.

"Or...untoolworthy," he rambled, making a reference to my habit of regularly breaking his tools.

"That's not a word. And no one's ever called me that."

"Well, I'm sure someone thinks it."

"Who?" I dared him to answer, knowing full well he was referring to himself. That's why he keeps his shed locked and equipped with an electronic alarm.

"Doesn't matter who. I'm just using all these words as random name-calling examples."

I sighed. "Can we get to the encouragement part?"

Then he said something that was actually helpful.

"Ya know, the Bible says Christians are blessed when they're perse-cuted. So maybe you should stop thinking of it as being insulted for 12 minutes and start thinking of it as being blessed."

I paused to consider what he said before responding, "You should have led with that."

"Well, next time."

That caught me off guard again. "Wait! You think there'll be a next time that I'm called names?"

"You've got a mirror," Rob replied without thinking.

"*What!?*"

Rob sensed that he had just stepped on a land mine. "Yeah, I'm not good at this. You wanna pray?"

We always pray whenever one of us is about to get on a flight, so I said, "Father God, I ask you to surround Rob with your angels and give him traveling mercies as he flies home. Give him an empty seat next to him so he can sleep, or place a person there that you want him to talk to. Just be more careful in choosing Rob's seat partner than Rob was in choosing his fat, ugly, stupid words. And please forgive him for thinking I'm untoolworthy. In Jesus's name, Amen."

"Amen," Rob said. "You think you're funny, don't ya?"

"A little. By the way, I broke your saw."

CLICK!

I tried to get back to sleep, but I kept running that podcast through my mind. I caught myself and tried to concentrate on what Rob had said instead. He's right. When we're pursuing God's call in our lives, we should expect resistance. And obstacles. And even hatred. But when the attacks come, and they will, we shouldn't retreat. We should keep running the good race, even with the "BOOM, BOOMs" resounding in our ears.

The thought comforted me, but I still couldn't get back to sleep. I turned the light on and grabbed my Bible and read, "In the shelter of your presence you hide them from all human intrigues; you keep them safe in your dwelling from accusing tongues. Praise be to the LORD, for he showed me the wonders of his love when I was in a city under siege" (Psalm 31:20-21).

Reading that passage brought me back to high school, where I definitely felt like a city under siege. I thought those were the wasted years of my life, but as it turned out, those were the years that God redeemed. I may not have been a Christian at the time, but He was already planting the seeds of who I would become. Being ostracized and alone, I developed an observational eye and an ear for dialogue— both qualities that serve me well today in my writing. I also developed my love for acting because I so badly wanted to be anybody but Boom-Boom.

I was reminded of the first time I had lunch with Bible scholar Kay Arthur, and how I was amazed that she kept calling me "beloved." *Why would she call you that?* said the voices from my past. *You're not beloved. You're Boom-Boom!*

When I asked Kay about it, she said, "Well, that's what God calls you, so that's what I'm gonna call you too. That's who you are. You're God's beloved."

"Beloved" is a healing word, acting as a salve for any word-scars we carry. I just need to remember to keep renewing my prescription for that particular salve, so that when people try to tear me down, I can keep reminding myself that God sees me (and you) as His beloved. God doesn't define me by my weight, my career, my success, my politics, or any other of a million things. I'm defined by my relationship with God. And you are too.

No bully is big enough to stand between you and what God wants to achieve through you. If enduring jokes about my appearance is the worst thing that ever happens to me, I think I'm pretty fortunate.

I closed the Bible and turned off my light, feeling comforted. I realized that I needed the Word not just in the morning, but also before I went to sleep. I vowed that from that point on, I wanted the last words I heard before surrendering to slumber to come from my Beloved.

To make sure I remembered this important moment, I rewrote the lyrics to a familiar tune, and it goes like this: "Look at me, I'm Torry De. Blessed through all eternity. Won't go to bed till I'm spiritually fed. I can't! I'm Torry De!"

3
GETTING MY GOAT

 man covered in blood burst into the high school journalism class and bellowed, "I got a fresh kill!" The students stared back in stunned silence.

The short man, about five and a half feet tall and weighing a little over 130 pounds, scanned the room before yelling, "I need my boy! Touchdown!"

I was in the adjoining room working on some ad copy when I heard the word "Touchdown." Trying to keep my composure, I walked into the main classroom and saw him standing there. "Hi, Dad. Bad day at the office?"

"C'mon!" he said to me. "I just killed a bear! We gotta get your brother."

Ah, so it was *bear* blood on his clothes! Everyone breathed a sigh of relief. He might have explained that little detail sooner to remove any fear that he was a crazed serial killer on the loose.

My father was clearly pumped up on adrenaline as he hurried me out of the classroom and into the hallway.

"I was out huntin' for deer, but I accidentally got caught between a mama bear and her cubs!" he said before lowering his voice and adding, "The last place you want to be."

29

Acting out the story, my dad stood in front of a locker and continued. "The mama bear was only 15 feet away from me, and I saw her sizing me up. I didn't want to kill her, but if she charged, I was gonna have to."

Dad raised an invisible rifle to his shoulder and pointed it at me.

"Just as I trained my gun on her, she growled, lowered her head, and BOOM!" my father shouted, slamming his back against the locker. "I dumped her!"

A hall monitor came around the corner just as the words "I dumped her" came out of my father's mouth. The monitor stopped dead in his tracks and took one look at my blood-covered father and then at me, as if seeking an explanation.

"Bad breakup with a girlfriend," I joked, nodding my head in my father's direction. The monitor didn't stick around to ask any more questions and scurried off down the hall.

My father said he had skinned and cut up the bear, explaining that it had taken him a whole half hour to lug just one hunk of bear meat up to the house. Realizing he was going to need help, he did what any insane, red-blooded American father would do. He leaped into his pickup truck and raced to the high school to pull his two teenage boys out of class and bring them home to help carry the carnivore up the canyon. He knew he needed to move the bear meat before it spoiled. He didn't have time to waste.

My brother, Tracy, was in gym class, so as I led the way, I said, "The PE teacher doesn't like anyone leaving early, even if they say they have to attend the funeral of their favorite uncle. Not that I've ever done that. Anyway, to get him out of class, you're really gonna have to sell it, Dad. You've gotta be convincing, so show some range. Go big-small-big."

"Big-small-big?" he said. My father never asked for acting tips, but this was my area of expertise.

"Yeah. Start with a dramatic 'Help,' and then stand there for a sec and let them think you're an escaped kidnap victim. Then go small and quiet. Say, 'I just need some help.' Then go big again by screaming, 'I killed a bear! I need my boy!'"

I stood outside the gym while my dad rushed inside and put on the performance of his life. He even improvised a few lines: "Let's go, Tracy! Tonight we're having bear stew!" The words "bear stew" echoed off the gymnasium walls.

My dad exited the gym, followed close behind by my diminutive brother, who was about the same size as my dad and was dressed from head to toe in all-white gym clothes.

"How'd I do?" my dad asked.

"Oscar worthy," I said. Then, gesturing toward my father's blood-covered clothing, I told Tracy, "You might want to change out of the white."

He gave me a withering look that only a brother could give. Then we jumped in my dad's pickup and raced home.

"Slow down!" Mr. Stanky yelled.

"Mow your lawn!" my dad called back.

We found the dead bear in the canyon behind our house, and Tracy and I had to work together to carry the bloody, slippery, heavy meat. We kept dropping it as we fought our way up the steep slope. Climbing uphill from the canyon was tough enough empty-handed, let alone while trying to lug a bloody carcass. We worked together for several hours, carrying portions of the carcass from the canyon to the house. By the end of it, we looked like extras in a Quentin Tarantino revenge film.

I love my dad. He's a colorful character, and he's the type of guy who would give you the shirt off his back. On top of his job as the produce manager of a grocery store, he has an assortment of hobbies, like hunting, gold mining, taxidermy, and watching football.

My dad *loves* football, which was why he'd given me the nickname Touchdown on the day I was born. He dreamed his bouncing baby boy would one day play the sport. Unfortunately, this big baby would only bounce. Poor guy wanted a quarterback but got a Quarter

Pounder instead. Some dreams never die though, and the nickname
has stuck. He and Mom even crafted my initials around this nickname by making sure that I would be T. D. Martin, as in Touchdown
Martin. That's how my official name became Torry De Martin, with
the middle name "De" spelled with only one "e" for some inexplica-
ble reason. Seriously, nurse at the hospital, how hard is it to spell "Dee"
correctly on a birth certificate? Even a high school journalism student
would have caught that one.

Imagine my dad's disappointment when he learned that his son,
T. D. Martin, couldn't care less about football and was incompetent
in all sports. To me, T. D. stands for "Tastes Delicious."

But hunting wild animals in our backyard was just the tip of my
dad's iceberg of eccentricity. I'll never forget my sixteenth birthday,
when he told me to close my eyes because he had a gift waiting for me
outside in the driveway.

Any boy who is told on his sixteenth birthday that there's a gift in
the driveway instinctively knows it's a car. Was it a Ford Mustang? A
Dodge Ram? A Volkswagen Rabbit?

It was a goat. I'm not sure what year or model.

My jaw dropped.

"I got him playing pool!" my father said proudly.

"Did you lose?"

"You look disappointed," he said, noting my lack of enthusiasm.

"I was expecting a car."

"Naw, this is better than a car. It has *two* horns—*and* it runs on
grass!"

I stared at him blankly as he laughed at his own joke. I was glad
one of us found it amusing.

"I'm gonna call him Billy," I said.

"Why do you want to give him my name?" he asked.

"So I'll always know who to thank," I replied sarcastically. Besides, I
had a feeling I was going to butt heads with this goat as much as I did
with my father. Seemed appropriate.

I also tried fishing for some sympathy from my mom about getting a goat instead of a car, but she didn't take the bait.

"With your grades, you should be grateful you got anything at all," she said. "That goat will teach you responsibility. Besides, I think he's kind of cute."

I hated that goat, and soon I wouldn't be alone in my loathing.

Three weeks later, my mom was headed out to her car in the morning and was surprised to hear bleating coming from somewhere above her head. She was stunned by what she saw. Mom marched back into the house and told my dad, "You need to see something."

"What?"

"I want it to be a surprise."

Our curiosity piqued, my dad followed her outside, as did Tracy and I. When we looked up, our jaws dropped in unison.

Our goat was 12 feet up in a tree.

Until this moment, I had no idea that goats could even climb trees. But climbing is what they do best. The scary part was that Billy the Goat had gotten his rope tangled on a couple of big branches, and Billy the Dad was afraid that if our ornery pet fell from the tree, he might strangle himself.

After my dad climbed the tree and unclipped the rope, Tracy, Mom, and I tried calling up to Billy the Goat to coax him down. But this goat was no dummy. He knew that if he came down, he'd immediately be tied back up. To avoid this, he climbed onto a higher branch, which placed him directly above the shed. From there he jumped down on the shed and walked to the peak, where he stood as still as a statue. He looked like a giant goat weathervane or one of Santa's rejected reindeer.

Undaunted, my dad grabbed a ladder and leaned it against the shed, figuring he had the goat trapped. But the sound of the ladder clanging against the building scared the goat, so it ran to the edge of the shed and did a quick goat parkour, landing squarely on the roof of my mom's car and leaving nice little dents with its hooves.

"Billy! Get down!" my mom shouted, but I wasn't sure if she was mad at the goat or blaming my father. My father wasn't sure either, so he scrambled down the ladder in case it was him.

My mom ran toward the goat, yelling and waving her arms, and this scared the goat so much that it jumped from the dented roof to the hood of the car, leaving another set of dents.

"Billy! Do something!" she screamed. (This time I was pretty sure she was talking to my dad.)

"Stop yelling!" my dad yelled. "You're scaring him. Stay calm and talk to him nicely, and he'll hop down on his own."

My dad demonstrated how to calm the goat, saying in a soothing tone, "Come here, you silly little Billy. It's okay."

That seemed to do the trick, and Billy jumped from the car hood, landing not far from me. So I inched forward, saying quietly, "We're not going to hurt you, buddy."

"I am!" my mother yelled. "I'm gonna kill him!"

My mother lunged for the goat. But after hearing Mom's death threat, the goat decided to seek safety by leaping back onto the hood of the car, up to the roof of the car, and then back onto the roof of the shed, leaving a trail of fresh dents along the way.

Billy the Goat wanted to be as far from Mom as possible, and I didn't blame him. If you ever saw my mom mad, you'd head for the nearest rooftop too.

My dad scrambled back up the ladder as fast as he could to capture the goat. But the critter spied the blood in my father's eyes and once again jumped from the top of the shed to the roof of the car, then again to the hood, and to the ground, where my brother and I finally caught him.

I looked at my father proudly. "Whaddya know—I finally made a touchdown!"

"Uhhh…it's technically a tackle. But still, nice play!"

My mother was less impressed. She would have to drive the dented vehicle to work.

"Look at my car! What am I gonna tell people?" she gasped, staring at the dents in her Chevy Nova.

"You could tell 'em one of your 'kids' did it," I said.

My mom just fumed. "I hate that goat."

"Really?" I said. "I think he's kinda cute."

After my mom hopped in her car and peeled out of the driveway, I turned to my dad. "How would you feel if we regifted the goat to someone more deserving?"

He thought for a moment before responding. "Not a bad idea actually. And I think I've got someone in mind."

"Who?"

* * * * * * * * *

It was just after midnight with a sliver of moon in the sky when four Martins crept through the Stankys' yard. My dad and brother drove a stake into the ground while I held the goat and my mom served as a lookout.

"If Stanky won't mow his lawn, I will," my dad said. He then turned to the goat and corrected himself. "I mean, *you* will."

Before leaving, my family turned back to admire our work. "Stanky, you've just been Martinized," my dad said proudly.

Later, when we drove by the Stankys' yard, I waved at Billy, and my Mom scolded me. "Don't wave at him! They'll know it was us."

Another time, just to annoy my mother, I saw Biff in the yard with the goat, and I yelled out the window, "His name's Billy!"

My mom floored it.

* * * * * * * * *

The goat was just one in a long line of peculiar pets. Once, we went to Pennsylvania, and my dad decided his boys needed a pet skunk— yes, a pet *skunk*—so he purchased one there (at the skunk store?), and we planned to carry it 2,595 miles in the car home to Washington.

The purpose of the pet purchase was to keep my brother and me from fighting in the backseat, and it worked. No one wanted to move in fear that we would set off the stink bomb. We named him Mr. Stanky in honor of our neighbor and for the impression he made on our car. Over the course of our journey, we bonded as I held him in my lap from Ohio to South Dakota. When we approached Mount Rushmore, my dad wanted me to get out to see the monument, but I didn't want to disturb Mr. Stanky's sleep.

"Are you gonna get out of the car and join us?" Dad asked.

"They're men carved in stone, Dad, they're not going anywhere. Besides, Mr. Stanky's sleeping. I don't want to bother him."

"Mr. Stanky's been asleep for a really long time," Tracy observed.

Dad came over to investigate further and shared the sad news. "I hate to tell you boys this, but Mr. Stanky's dead."

"That stinks," Tracy said.

"Too early," my dad noted. "But good one."

I was devastated, and my semi-sensitive dad tried to comfort me the only way a taxidermist knew how. "I could stuff him if you like."

"No. That's okay."

"How about I clip his tail, and we can sew it on a hat?"

"Nooo. I'm good."

We buried the skunk facing Mount Rushmore's Lincoln. My dad worried that Mr. Stanky wouldn't rest in peace unless he was facing a Republican.

We also had a pet duck, which was completely useless when it came to playing fetch. However, the duck was mysteriously released in the middle of the night by someone who looked exactly like me but hasn't confessed yet. And then there was the pet raccoon named Rocky, which was just the right word to describe the raccoon's tumultuous relationship with my mother. We kept Rocky in Dad's garage, but one time it got into the house and trapped my mom in the kitchen, where she had to stand on a chair to keep from getting bit. Every time she tried to get off of the chair, that raccoon would get up on its hind legs and start hissing like a demon. She was stuck on the chair for 45 minutes until my dad got home from work.

We eventually got rid of the raccoon when it decided to expand its diet plan by adding my dad's thumb to the menu. It bit the thumb halfway off, and the digit had to be sewn back on. When he was young, my dad used that thumb to hitchhike from Washington to Pennsylvania to tell his mother he had proposed to a lovely young lady named Verna. So he really wanted to keep the thumb for sentimental reasons, if nothing else.

On the way to the hospital, I tried to cheer up my father, just in case they couldn't save his opposable digit. "You could use your taxidermy skills and turn it into a key ring."

"No. That's okay," he said.

"I could sew it to the top of your baseball hat. Then you could hitchhike to Grandma's without ever raising your hand."

"Nooo. I'm good."

My dad meant well with his wacky gifts, but he didn't really know what his son wanted. After all, we were from two different worlds. He loved football, hunting bears, and stuffing raccoons, while I loved theater and cooking, where the only things I ever stuffed were green peppers.

* * * * * * * * *

Even though we all have fallible fathers here on earth, it's comforting to know we have a Father in heaven, and He has given each one of us gifts that are specifically suited to us. It's not a question of *whether* you have a gift and a calling. We all have a calling. The challenge is discovering what your gift and calling might be and being content with whatever that is.

It took me a while to learn that not everyone has the same gift. This may seem obvious, but a lot of us, myself included, wish we could have a white-elephant exchange. "Here, take my gift. I like yours better."

I spent much of my life suffering from a severe case of comparative-worthitis—wanting to be anybody but me. I envied other people's gifts because I didn't think I had any of my own. (Water retention isn't really a gift.) But as Romans 12:6 says, "We have different gifts, according to the grace given to each of us."

When I was living in my cabin in Alaska, I remember listening to a televangelist, and someone asked him, "What if we *don't* exercise our spiritual gifts?" The evangelist responded by saying that using our gifts is a matter of obedience, and that failing to do so could adversely affect the body of Christ.

That was a sobering thought, and that message became a turning point in my Christian life. It led me to finally take seriously the matter of responding to my calling.

Our earthly fathers may offer us goats, skunks, and unwanted advice on how to throw a perfect spiral, but the gifts we receive from God are designed specifically for us. And we should thank Him for them daily.

After all, with Him, every day is Father's Day.

BLOODLINES. I don't know if my dad was more proud to pose with his two sons or to show off the bear blood on his left leg. This is when my brother, Tracy, and I were in high school.

FOREST FASHION. I told my dad I needed a new hat, so he took us shopping in the woods.

SON OF A TAXIDERMIST. I'm still getting my wardrobe from the wilderness—or in this case, from the roadside. Rob and I had a small business making fur hats and bikinis entirely from roadkill. Our fashion line was called "Accidental Clothing," and our motto was "You'll stop them dead in their tracks." The hat on my head in this photo was made from a fox that had apparently been a hit-and-run victim in Alaska.

4

NOT-SO-SWEET SIXTEEN

eing in high school was like being a kid forced to take up the tuba. It's terrible for the child but way worse for the parents.

I can hardly believe what my mom and dad put up with during those years when I was a human hurricane of rebellious behavior. While other parents had bumper stickers proudly proclaiming, "My child is an honor student," I was driving my car into those bumpers. Not that it made much difference to the vehicle I was driving. My mother got a new car, and I got a hand-me-down from a goat—the banged-up Billy-mobile.

During my senior year, I started to drink heavily, and in one instance, I struck three cars in the span of a minute. I was going less than five miles an hour when I tapped the car in front of me at a stoplight. Panicking, I put the car in reverse and tapped the car behind me, giving me just enough space to pull forward into the next lane, where I tapped the car beside me. I tried to flee the scene, but a policeman witnessed the whole thing and chased me down for about two miles. I was charged with a DUI and three hit and runs, was fined close to $1,000, and spent 48 hours in jail.

It was enough to drive a person to drink. (Yes, I know that was an irreverent joke, but humor is my way of dealing with a subject I'm hesitant to bring up. I was only 16 when the DUI happened, and it disappeared from my record, so people don't know about it. But I'm sharing it now because there might be some readers who are raising a Torry-type delinquent and are about to give up. My hope is to give hope to those who feel hopeless. And oh, what the heck, for those who need even more hope, I'll share a little more.)

Another time, I was inebriated when I ran a stop sign at an intersection where the only options were to turn right or left. I went with the third option and drove straight ahead, off the road, and wound up suspended in the top of a tree. I tried to put the car in reverse even though the vehicle was about 20 feet off the ground. (Don't try this at home. Air doesn't have much traction.) Then there was the time I drove my father's '57 Chevy pickup into the corner of our house so hard that it knocked my brother out of his bed. A few weeks later, I drove the pickup into a double flowering plum tree in full bloom. I was high at the time and wanted a closer look.

Alcohol was only part of the picture. I also experimented with acid, speed, and cocaine, but marijuana was my drug of choice. To me, higher learning meant going to school stoned. I was a dedicated pot smoker, and I partially credit the munchies for my body size.

One time I spent all my money on pot and came home stoned to raid the fridge. My dad smelled the pot on me and made me empty my jacket pockets in front of him. He found the joint and lectured me for 20 minutes. All I could think was, *When will this be over? You're ruining my high—and you're blocking the pantry.* When his lecture finally ended, he said, "Do you have anything to say for yourself?"

"Yeah," I responded. "Do we have any Doritos?"

Grounded for a month. No Doritos for a year.

The drugs and alcohol helped me escape reality, and as far as I was concerned, my reality needed escaping from. I didn't have many friends in high school until I became a stoner, and even those friendships were conditional. They only stayed my friends if I supplied the pot and the car to go get it.

Substance abuse became my extracurricular activity, and my school activities were no better. Or should I say, my school inactivities, because I was hardly ever there. As a result, in my final semester of high school, I was not going to graduate unless I took a night class at Olympic College in Washington. A *night* class? I had a hard enough time staying awake in class during the *day*.

My brother was a stellar student and graduated without any problems at all, so my mom said she wasn't about to have her other son fail to graduate high school. To make certain of that, she made the excruciating announcement that she was going to be taking the night class *with* me!

I could imagine the scene immediately:

TEACHER: Okay, who can give me an example of how a bill becomes a law? Yes, Verna.

MY MOM: Let's say I wanted to make it a federal law that my son Torry here washes inside his ears when he takes a bath...

ME: Mom!

MY MOM: I would write the bill and send it to the Congressional Committee for Basic Decency and Properly Acting like a Grown Adult.

TEACHER: Very good, Verna. Then what?

MY MOM: I'd have him arrested right now.

TEACHER (*looking closely at my ears*): Oh, you're right. Look, class! Look at Torry's ears!

CLASS: Ewww!

My mom and I were pulling out of the driveway to head to our first class when she said, "I just don't know what's wrong with you. You should be enjoying high school. These are the best years of your life!"

She continued driving, but I slammed on the brakes in my head and thought, "THESE are the best years of *my life*?"

Leaning my head against the window, I stared out as we drove 30 more minutes to the college in complete silence. It gave me a lot of time to think. I may have been brainless, but I wasn't heartless. I knew this was as hard on my mom as it was on me. The last thing she wanted was to attend this class with me after working her full-time job.

When we arrived in the college parking lot, I decided to apologize to her. "I'm sorry, Mom. I don't know what's wrong with me either. I'm going to try to change. I promise."

"Good."

"Can you do me a favor though? I don't want anyone to know you're my mom. So when we're in class, can I just call you Verna?"

My mom stared back at me for a moment. "As long as you graduate, you can call me anything you want." So the deal was struck.

I walked into class first, and my mom waited a few seconds before she followed me into the room. Then she sat down in the seat directly across from me and said, "Hi, I'm Verna!"

"Hi. I'm Torry. Nice to meet you."

She then looked at the side of my head, because my hair had become mushed from leaning it for 30 minutes against the car window. Unable to control herself, she gave her fingers a quick lick and reached over to smooth my hair.

I immediately pulled back and shouted, "Mom!"

We blew our cover in 15 seconds. Turning bright red with embarrassment, I could see the confused expressions on the faces of the students around me. The guy on the other side of me gave me a sympathetic look.

"Welcome to the best years of my life," I muttered to him.

Of all things, the class I had to make up was psychology. Can you imagine a worse subject to study with your *mother*? The day we were studying Freud, I turned to my mom and exclaimed in the middle of class, "I finally know what's wrong with me! You! It's all your fault!"

As the comedian Robin Williams once said, "Freud: If it's not one thing, it's your mother."

In high school, my primary study strategy was to sit next to the smartest people in class and copy their work. My mom was one of the smartest people in this class, but she kept her arms curled around her paper like the Great Wall of Verna.

I was sleeping in class one day when she whispered, "Torry, wake up! Torry De!"

I pretended I didn't hear her. A second later, I was nailed in the head with a spit wad. I already had enough of her saliva in my hair, so I raised my hand and told the teacher, "She keeps talking to me. Could you please move her?"

"Verna, would you mind moving to the back of the class?" the teacher asked.

Ohhh, the look she gave me. You could microwave a TV dinner with the heat from her eyes. Without flinching, she calmly got out of her chair, leaned over to me, and very sweetly whispered in her most ominous Clint Eastwood voice, "I'll be watching you."

Moving Mom to the back of the room was in some ways worse. All throughout class, I could feel her eyes boring through me. I felt like I had one of those sniper laser dots dancing on my back.

The very next class, as we entered the room, my mom motioned toward the back row and jokingly asked, "Should I sit back here?"

She was surprised when I said yes.

She reluctantly took the seat in the back row, and I could tell I hurt her feelings. So I said, "Mind if I take the seat next to you?"

"Sure," she smiled.

I then leaned over and whispered, "Besides, we can sleep back here, and the teacher will never notice."

Instantly, my five-foot mom shot out of her desk, latched onto my arm, dragged me directly to the front row, and pushed me into a seat. "You. Will. Graduate!"

Thanks to that class, I did manage to squeak by and graduate from high school—much to the shock of everyone, especially my math teacher. He hated me, and he didn't make it a secret. I hated math, and I didn't make that a secret either.

I also hated the desks in his class. Clearly they were designed for underfed elves. It took a shoehorn and a squirt of WD-40 just to get me into one. Once, when I was attempting to squeeze into my desk, my math teacher said out loud in front of the class, "Torry, if you stop adding Twinkies to your body equation, you might be able to subtract some from your middle."

The only thing worse than math is math humor.

On the last day of class, he went through the roster of students, one by one, and shared his bright expectations for their future.

"Marie, I expect you to go to college and become a doctor," he said proudly. "Biff, I think you'll be a pro football player. Megan, you'll make a wonderful teacher."

And then he came to me.

My teacher stared at me for a few moments before letting out a big sigh and saying the six most devastating words I had heard in all my years of schooling.

"Torry, from you I expect nothing."

It felt like a thousand-pound weight had just dropped on all of my hopes and dreams. That teacher's words became implanted in my mind, and from that point on, I didn't expect anything from myself either.

Contrast that math teacher with Karyn Lackman, who was hands down the best teacher I ever had. She taught English and ended each class five minutes early, giving students free time to work on their own. During those five minutes, she would call one student up to her desk to get to know them and give them individual encouragement.

I'll never forget when she called me up for the five-minute talk. She told me how much she liked my latest journal entry and how creative and funny I was. As I returned to my seat, I was glowing. I, Torry "Boom-Boom" Martin, had just received a compliment from Ms. Lackman, the most popular teacher at our high school!

Ms. Lackman was my academic lifeboat, keeping me afloat when my dreams of success had been torpedoed. She was also the one who first got me interested in writing. She required us to keep journals— the one thing I actually put my heart and soul into. "You have a keen observational eye," she told me. "You notice the details in life that most people overlook, and you do it in a humorous way."

I lived off that compliment for days, and it inspired me to write better. I wanted to please Ms. Lackman more than anything, and I loved having an outlet to vent my thoughts during the turmoil of my high school years. In fact, I probably loved writing in my journal too much, because I would keep writing in it during all of my classes when I was supposed to be concentrating on other subjects.

Ms. Lackman was my Barnabas.

• • • • • • • • •

Barnabas is one of my favorite characters in the Bible. His name actually means "Son of Encouragement," and he certainly lived up to it.

When the apostle Paul first tried to join the disciples to spread the Good News of Jesus Christ, the believers were terrified of him. After all, Paul had gone to great lengths to persecute the followers of Jesus. He was even there when Stephen became the church's first martyr.

So what did Barnabas do? He accompanied Paul when visiting the disciples, vouching for him and telling everyone about Paul's conversion. Paul went on to turn the world upside down by spreading the gospel. But we often forget that it took an encourager like Barnabas to get him rolling and give him credibility in the eyes of the fledgling church.

Encouragement is the lifeblood that keeps our calling from God alive and thriving, so look for the Barnabases in your life, and *be* the Barnabas in the lives of others. You can learn about the power of encouragement in a psychology class, but better yet, just put it into practice right where you're at, starting with the people around you. And if you need someone to keep you in line and make sure you follow through on this assignment, I can loan my mom to you for a small fee.

She'll be watching you. But be careful. She's a spitter.

SPITTING IMAGE. Behind every mountain man is his mountain mama.

HIGHER LEARNING. This was supposed to be my secret stoner sweat-shirt—"High" Voltage. My dad saw right through it. He should be wearing a shirt that says, "Short Fuse."

PARENT TRAP. It doesn't matter how old I am...my parents still have the ability to take me out to the woodshed. (I love these little Martin munchkins!)

5

KILLING TOTO

I was an actor in my midtwenties looking for any kind of professional experience, so I was thrilled when I landed the role of the Cowardly Lion in the Seattle Center House Theater's production of *The Wizard of Oz*.

Playing the role of the Cowardly Lion gave me plenty of opportunity to ham it up—and if there are two things I love, it's excessive cowardice and ham (especially honey-glazed). My favorite scene was the one where the Cowardly Lion, acting oh so brave, runs after Toto. That's when Dorothy steps in to protect her dog by slapping the Cowardly Lion, and the big scaredy-cat starts blubbering and dabbing his eyes with his tail. *Finally, a role where I can show some range.* There was only one problem. They couldn't find a proper dog to play Toto in all of Seattle.

A few days into rehearsals, the director called a meeting to introduce us to our newest cast member. She had finally found a Toto.

I saw my director holding a picnic basket, but there was no sign of my new costar. *Where's Toto?*

As if on cue, a terrier popped his head out of the basket. Now I was really confused.

"He's a puppet?" I said.

"Woof! Woof!" the puppet replied in a high-pitched voice supplied by our fearless leader. "Your talented director stayed up aaaall night to make me!"

Talking about yourself in the third person is always odd. But talking about yourself in the third person *through a puppet*? That's flat-out weird. I looked at my director to make sure she hadn't lost her mind. But she was too busy talking in Toto's voice to notice my puzzlement.

"First, your director cut a hole in the side of this picnic basket, and then she sewed my puppet body on the inside!" Toto said. "Now, whenever Dorothy needs me, all she has to do is stick her hand in the basket to make me pop up, and ta-da! I'm here!"

The director turned Toto's head as if the dog were awaiting the reaction of the entire cast. We were all too stunned to respond.

"What do you think?" Toto asked, glancing around for approval.

"I think you're a basket case," I said without thinking.

"What?" my director snapped, using her own voice.

"Not you," I said, trying to assure her while simultaneously covering for my mistake. "I was talking to Toto."

My director didn't look convinced, so I tried to change the subject. "How am I supposed to do a chase scene with a puppet? I don't think it's gonna work."

I awaited my director's response, but Toto responded instead.

"Oooh, what's the matter, Cowardly Lion?" Toto taunted. "Are you *afraid* to act with a puppet? Are you *scared* I'll steal the scene? That's it, isn't it! You're nothing but a great big sissy-wissy, chubby-wubby *scaredy-cat*!"

SUH-WAP!

It took a second to register that I had just slapped a puppet.

As a method actor, I was completely in character, and I forgot that my director's hand was inside the puppet until she stumbled back a step.

I still don't know why I smacked the puppet. I guess I just snapped. Being bullied by Biff in high school was one thing, but getting teased by a terrier was where I drew the line. In all my life, I'd never defended myself from a bully, and I never would have tried with Biff. He was six foot three and 180 pounds of solid muscle. Since Toto was only twelve inches tall and didn't have teeth, I guess I figured I could take him.

Regardless, I was just as shocked by what I had done as everyone else.

My director checked the puppet's head to make sure he was okay before unleashing her full fury. "You're lucky you didn't hurt him! I stitched him by hand, and it took me all night!"

"How long would it take ya to stitch his lips?" I said sarcastically.

The cast laughed at my joke, but the director wasn't having it. "It would be in your best interest to apologize immediately, Mr. Martin. An actor is easily replaced. This puppet is not."

Oh, brother. I didn't even slap him that hard. It was just a tiny tap.

Being in the arts, the director was given to melodrama and was turning this into a big deal. The entire cast stood still, waiting to see what I would do.

"I'm sorry," I said quietly to my director, feeling like an idiot.

"Don't tell me. Tell *him*," she said, shoving the Toto basket in my face.

I thought she was joking, and I was just about to laugh until I saw "that look" in her eyes. Her glare said very clearly, "I'm dead serious."

"I'm…sorry—" I said to her again before remembering to quickly lower my eyes to the puppet and finish the sentence. "Toto. Will you please forgive me?"

"Woof-woof!" Toto's high-pitched voice responded.

"That means yes," my director informed me in her own voice. "And you can't see it right now, but inside this basket his tail is wagging!" She gave me a friendly smile that quite frankly made me a little nervous.

"Thank you, Toto," I replied, then leaned down and whispered, "Feel free to lift your leg while you're in there."

"Okay then! Everyone take a five-minute break except Dorothy, the Lion, and Toto. I want to walk through their choreography."

The plan was for me to leap out of the trees with a ferocious roar and grab for the basket. I would pull on it, and Dorothy would yank back. Then I'd tug on the basket again, but Dorothy would dig in her heels and pull back. On Dorothy's second tug, my hand would purposely slip off the basket, and Toto would finally be free. To cap it, Dorothy would set the basket down, step toward me, and give me a good hard stage slap right on the snout.

Perfect plan.

Things calmed down for our dress rehearsal that day, but little did I know that toward the end of our theatrical run, my little slap on the snout was going to seem frivolous compared to the canine homicide that was about to happen.

Busloads of second and third graders had been brought over from the local schools to see our matinee production. It was an intimate theater, with a stage that rose from the floor by only a foot. The front row was about four feet from the stage, which can pose a problem with an audience of unruly children.

When we reached the chase scene, Dorothy and I began our Toto tug-of-war, with me pulling on the basket and Dorothy yanking back. But when I went for my final pull, the unthinkable happened. My hand slipped from the basket handle, and I accidentally yanked Toto's head with such force that it completely came off.

The children gasped. *I had just decapitated Toto.*

Dorothy and I stood together in shock as Toto's severed head dangled from my paw. The audience went deathly quiet, but only for a moment. As a general rule, chaos follows carnage.

"HE KILLED TOTO!" one child shouted.

"NOOO!" screamed another.

Dorothy was no help. She had turned her back, trying to hide a giggle fit. If ruby slippers came in a size 13, I'd be clicking them all the way to Kansas.

"Get him, Dorothy!" a high-pitched voice yelled from the crowd.

"Beat him with your basket!"

"Kick him with your slippers!"

A couple of third graders geared up to rush the stage.

I stood there frozen, eyes wide in horror, as the screams of these snack-sized rioters filled the theater. It was clear. These grade-school munchkins were the Lollipop Kids, and I was the sucker. Sweat poured down my face, and it had nothing to do with my overheated Cowardly Lion costume.

I was afraid they were planning to mount my head in the Wicked Witch's parlor or have Auntie Em use my hide as a throw rug. Personally, I'd prefer to be mounted on the wall—at least then I would have a nice view of things. Being a rug, I would just be splayed out in front of the fireplace and only see the spots that needed a good cleaning. But with my OCD, I would have been frustrated because I couldn't dust it myself. Then again...

Sorry, just caught myself in an ADHD/OCD tangent. Where was I?

Ah yes...my impending trampling. I felt like Quasimodo surrounded by a mob of angry villagers. Three hundred grade school children were poised to grab their pitchforks and attack me. But I was a pro, and every theater veteran needs to know how to improvise when the unthinkable happens. I quickly shoved Toto's severed head back into the basket and loudly announced to the audience how I was going to fix this.

"Don't worry, kids, I know CPR!" (Disclaimer: This is not the recommended AMA treatment of a decapitated head.)

I leaned down and pretended to give mouth-to-mouth—or, snout-to-snout—resuscitation. I thought it was working until a voice screamed, "HE'S EATING TOTO!"

"Somebody stop him!" wailed another between sobs.

Still trying to control the situation, I pulled my head back from the basket, showing them that I hadn't bitten off so much as a whisker from Toto. Then Dorothy, who had finally gotten her giggling under control, brought sanity to the scene with some quick-thinking improvisation. She managed to insert her hand back into the puppet and use some exquisitely awful ventriloquism to make him bark to show he was okay.

"Toto, are you all right?" Dorothy asked.

"WOOF!"

"Are you sure?"

"WOOF! WOOF!"

Dorothy carefully placed the basket on the floor and said to the doggie, "Well then, after all of that, you need to take a nap." She carefully covered Toto with the picnic napkin, walked over to me, and let a dramatic pause linger between us.

Then she hauled off and gave me a really BIG slap.

"Bad lion!" she shouted.

"Bad Dorothy!" I wanted to shout back because she was supposed to give me a stage slap, which sounds like the real deal but doesn't hurt. But she was so distracted by all that was going on that she gave me a full-force REAL slap. Owie! Mama! It stung so sharply that for the first time I didn't have to ham it up with my blubbering. If I hadn't been wearing claws, I would've slapped her right back.

· · · · · · · · ·

The Christian life is a lot like being on stage with a live audience—highly rewarding but also terrifying. Trying to follow God's call is scary business because it's inevitable that you are going to fail—A LOT. Like actors, whose worst nightmare is forgetting their lines, Christians struggle with a fear of failure in the eyes of God, and we always have to be ready to improvise, regardless of what life sends our way. We have to trust God as our heavenly Director and remain committed to our role, even when things seem to be falling apart around us and we're about to be mobbed by a theater full of menacing munchkins.

The show must go on.

"Whoever fears the LORD walks uprightly," says Proverbs 14:2. Many Hebrew words are translated as "fear," and the meanings can run the gamut from uneasiness to terror. If you check your Hebrew lexicon (and if you're like me, you'll have five, all well worn from overuse), you may even find a photograph of me dressed in my Cowardly Lion costume and holding the severed head of Toto as an illustration of terror.

But one of the most common meanings of fear, when used with God, is awe or reverence. It's the kind of feeling you get when you are in the presence of something bigger or mightier than yourself—like an imposing redwood tree or a majestic lion striding across a savannah. Coming into the presence of God should be that overwhelming.

A real lion's roar is one of the most awesome sounds in the natural world and can be heard five miles away. The king of the beasts is easily the loudest of the big cats, with a roar that can reach 114 decibels from three feet away. This is 25 times louder than a gas-powered mower—although I never tested this because my mower instructions clearly say you should never mow a lawn anywhere near a roaring lion.

I've actually heard a lion roar at night, and it was enough to send a shiver up my spine. This is how we should feel when we hear the call of God in our lives. We should be awestruck because we're stepping into the presence of a King. It's like the scene from *The Wizard of Oz* when Dorothy, the Tin Man, the Scarecrow, and the Cowardly Lion approach the Great Oz with their knees knocking.

"'Should you not fear me?' declares the LORD. 'Should you not tremble in my presence?'" (Jeremiah 5:22).

The fear of God also makes me think of the classic scene in C.S. Lewis's *The Lion, the Witch, and the Wardrobe*, where Susan asks Mr. Beaver if Aslan, the great lion, is safe.

"'Safe?' said Mr. Beaver...'Who said anything about safe? 'Course he isn't safe. But he's good. He's the King, I tell you.'"

To drive home this point, the character Tirian later says, "He is not a tame lion."

It's true. The Lord is a good King, but He isn't a safe King in the sense that we can make Him bend to our will. We cannot make Him jump through hoops like a trained lion in a circus. When we're in trouble, however, we can count on Him to be at our side to defend us, tooth and claw.

But be warned: He is most definitely *not* tame.

THE GREAT TOTO TUSSLE. There are moments you remember all your life.

6

DASHING THROUGH THE SNOW

It was late October as Rob and I chugged up the twisty, treacherous roads leading to my family's cabin for one last gold-mining expedition before the snow fell. Our gold mine was located at one of the highest points in Washington State.

Beginning in the early 1980s, my family owned a one-eighth stake in the Golden Arrow mining claim. So when I was in my twenties, Rob and I would go up there to do some hard-rock mining and gold panning. It was a slice of heaven for someone like me, who enjoyed hanging out with his best friend and also loved his solitude and alone time with God. If you combined a week at a monastery with playing the lottery, that's gold mining—which I suppose makes me and Rob two monks with a gambling problem.

There were other mining claims in the area, but they were all minus their miners. At the end of October, we knew we were cutting it a little close by going up for one more mining trip before the snow shut everything down. We appeared to be the only souls crazy enough to make the trip this late.

Fine by me. I thrived on peace and quiet.

After parking the car, we brought in our gear, and I prepared some food as the sun went down and the darkness deepened. Our only light was a lantern I placed in the middle of the dining table, which was positioned by the window. As I sat down to a meal, I thought about how wonderful it was to be away from the rest of the world, so I let out a deep, satisfied sigh, glanced out the window, stared into the pitch-dark night—and SCREAMED!

A haggard face was plastered up against the glass, staring back at me.

Leaping to my feet, I backpedaled from the table. It took a few moments to realize it was just the wrinkly, unwashed face of Mel, an old man who pitched a tent in these parts and kept his eye on everything and everyone. Evidently he had seen our car coming up the mountain but didn't recognize it as belonging to my parents. So he decided to find out what was going on by hiking a couple of miles to our cabin and pressing his greasy nose against our window, nearly giving me a heart attack.

But then the real terror began. We had to listen to this old man tell old jokes for the next four hours. It was misery for everyone except Mel. He reveled in having a captive audience.

Mel popped in for dinner that night and the next because that's what Mel did. He would pitch a tent and show up at various miners' cabins to mooch food and tell his very limited supply of bad puns from the 1940s. I think his favorite comedy writer was Bazooka Joe.

"Do you know Mike?" he asked.

"Mike who?" I said.

"Mike country 'tis of thee."

He paused, waiting for a laugh. (There weren't any crickets in the cabin, but somewhere I heard a mouse groan.)

Undeterred, he continued. "Do you know Arthur?"

I refused to answer this time, but Rob caved.

"Arthur who?" Rob asked unenthusiastically.

"Arthurmometer."

And those were his *best* ones.

At dinner on the second night, Mel served us the same leftover jokes, so I was relieved when he informed us that he would be packing up and leaving the next morning. I remember closing the door after Mel left and turning to Rob to say, "Do you know Gladys?"

"Gladys who?"

"Gladys HeckMelisgone."

Washington's highest public road was Hart's Pass, where you could find a ranger station. But our mining claim was actually a few miles beyond Hart's Pass and could be reached only through a private gate. The mine was so remote that cell phones didn't work up there. (I didn't really mind though, because they hadn't been invented yet.) The nearest phone was at a gas station in the microscopic town of Mazama, but it took a good one and a half to two hours to reach it by car, following narrow, winding dirt roads.

The curve around Dead Horse Canyon was the most nerve-racking stretch on this road because only one car could drive along it at a time, and one side of the road was a sheer drop and sure death if you went over the edge. They named it Dead Horse Canyon because a long time ago some miners were leading a string of horses and wagons along the path, and one of the horses tumbled over the edge, taking several more down with it, along with a couple of miners and their wagon.

I usually kept my eyes closed whenever we went around the curve at Dead Horse Canyon. That was why Rob did the driving and I was in charge of the eye-closing.

As it turned out, we wound up having a good week of hard-rock mining. With lights mounted on our hard hats, we chipped away at a quartz vein in a tunnel that curved its way back about 120 feet into the mountain.

The day before we were scheduled to leave, we came out of the mine after working for a few hours and were shocked to see the ground blanketed with snow, and there were more flakes falling.

"We've gotta get out of here!" Rob said.

We raced to pack the car, and it wasn't until we had it fully loaded that we spotted two problems. Number one: a flat tire. Number two: no spare.

Right about now, I would've given anything to hear Mel tell one of his six Harry Truman jokes.

I wanted nothing more than to get out of there, but we had no idea where we'd find help. The ranger station at Hart's Pass was a couple of miles away, but since it was so late in the season, we probably wouldn't find anyone there. With Mazama a two-hour drive away, if we tried walking there we wouldn't reach it until spring.

The snow was steadily falling, and time was of the essence. So I did what any pioneer would have done in such a dire situation.

I decided to take a shower.

I was covered in dirt from working the mine, so I figured that if they found my frozen corpse up here, it might as well be clean. Of course, there was no running water in the cabin, so I collected freezing water from a nearby stream and heated it up on the woodstove. Then I filled a shower bag with the lukewarm water and hung it up. Gravity carried the water out the bottom of the bag and through the shower nozzle.

In the mountains, you learned to take really quick showers because it didn't take long for all the water to trickle out of the bag.

Of course, we couldn't just shower smack in the middle of the one-room cabin, or we'd have a big puddle to mop up. So we hung the shower bag right by the back door, which we kept open to allow the water to drain outside. But you have to realize one important caution about this back door. You never wanted to walk through it, because that first step was a doozy. If you stepped outside, you would plunge 20 feet to the rocks below. No one had ever bothered to build a deck in back.

The only place this door led was directly to your death. It's kind of like Dead Horse Canyon, except you died with vibrant, healthy hair. We always wore gripper slippers to avoid slipping on the soap and tumbling out the open door.

Occasionally, as I showered, I'd be able to see a hiker way off in the distance, trudging along the Pacific Crest Trail—a trail that ran all the way from Canada to Mexico—and I prayed that they didn't have binoculars. But even if I had spotted hikers on this day, they would've been too far away to hear any cries for help. Besides, we needed a driver, not a hiker. We needed someone with a car to carry our flat tire down the mountain to get it fixed in Winthrop—an additional half-hour beyond Mazama.

As I stood under the shower, praying for a miracle, I sighed and stared through the open door, lost in thought. Suddenly, right before my one open eye (the other one had shampoo in it), I spied a car crawling up the narrow road across the canyon! Mel had been the only other person we saw all week, and now a car appeared like a gift from heaven. Forgetting I was completely naked (except for my gripper slippers), I jumped up and down, waving my hands wildly, and shouting, "Hey! Hey! Hey!"

The jumping caused shampoo to drip into my other eye, blinding me completely. Feeling around for my towel, I ran for the front door and hit the wall twice before I found it and flung it open. Dashing through the snow, minus the sleigh, I shouted, "Rob! A car!"

Rob saw where I was pointing, pulled his .44 Magnum out of its holster, and unloaded three rounds into the ground—three being the signal for distress. He then paused and shot three more rounds in quick succession, hoping it would draw the man's attention. It wasn't working, so I ripped off my towel and waved it frantically, while yelling at the top of my lungs, "Hey! Over here!"

I know the guy saw me because he immediately sped up.

As the car disappeared, Rob glared at me. "You drove him away."

"You were the one shooting at him," I said. If there'd been any bullets left, Rob would've used them on me.

"I'll hike over and follow the car tracks and see if I can talk to the guy," Rob suggested. "You stay here."

"Where else am I going to go? My gripper slippers are frozen to the ground."

So Rob hiked down the hill, slipping and sliding in the snow every step of the way. He crossed the bridge to the other side of the canyon and followed the tire tracks until he reached the man's claim. It was a long hike, but I was still surprised that it took two hours for Rob to return. I was even more surprised when he came back driving the guy's car. I knew we were desperate, but grand theft auto? Didn't seem like Rob.

"He's closing his cabin for the season," Rob said, "so he loaned us his car to drive to Winthrop and get our tire fixed."

The fellow was incredibly generous, because loaning us the car would take hours. It must have been terribly inconvenient. The man also put himself at risk of being stranded if we didn't make it back before the snow completely closed the road. But it saved our skins. We had our tire fixed in Winthrop, filled the guy's car with gas, and made the long drive back with a freshly repaired spare and a fresh pepperoni pizza from Three-Fingered Jack's as a thank-you.

After returning the car, we changed our tire and took off for home. But on the way, we stopped at a pay phone, where I called my mom to tell her we were headed back. I also told her about the flat tire and how the guy saved us.

"Did you remember to tell him thank you?"

"No, Mom, we said, 'See ya later, sucka,' and drove off with his car." *I can't believe she asked me that.* "Of course we said thank you!" I assured her. "We also filled his tank and got him a pizza."

"Was it from Three-Fingered Jack's?"

Now she was questioning my proper pizza-purchasing ability? "No, Mom, it was frozen cheese."

"Torry De!" she exclaimed.

Did I remember to say thank you? Such a Mom thing to say.

•   •   •   •   •   •   •   •   •

The more I thought about it, however, the more I realized that it's a good reminder of what we often neglect to do with God. We often forget to say thank you to Him for the people He sends into our lives.

The folks God sends your way can be as astonishing as encountering a stranger with a car when you're trapped in a mountain cabin. As you pursue your calling, pay attention and you'll see that God often places just the right person in just the right place at just the right time. In fact, the people He puts in our path are like gold nuggets sprinkled throughout our lives, so keep your eyes peeled.

There's God in them thar hills.

TABLE MANNERS. The window to my left is where Mel rudely pressed his dirty face to the glass and scared me to death. (For a guy who knows so many knock-knock jokes, you'd think Mel would've used the door.)

GOLD FEVER! Yes, I know there's a sign warning that this gold mine is a hard-hat area. But since Rob and I are already both hardheaded, we felt we were sufficiently protected.

DEAD HORSE CANYON. One misstep here, and it's a plummet from the summit.

7

I HAD MY SPILL ON BLUEBERRY HILL

It was a gorgeous morning as I hiked up the steep hill dressed in my onesie Superman pajamas and rubber boots and carrying a bowl under my arm for collecting blueberries. Rob led the way while my mom stoked the woodstove back at the cabin and started cooking the bacon.

Before we left, my dad had warned us that the bacon was going to draw every bear in the area, so I made sure Rob was carrying his .44 Magnum. I disliked the idea of running into a bear, but I disliked the idea of pancakes without blueberries even more. Thankfully, those tasty tidbits flourished close to our cabin, so they'd be easy pickings.

In addition to bacon, bears love blueberries, and as we climbed the hill, Rob pointed out some bear scat that contained evidence of the little blue fruit.

"That looks fresh," he said. The last thing I wanted was to battle a bear over blueberries. The carnivores always have the upper claw. Now I was on high alert, looking for bears everywhere.

The side of the hill where we did our picking was nearly vertical—a great hill for sledding—and as I started gathering fruit, Rob told me he needed to make a trip to the outhouse.

"I'll be right back," he said. "Make sure you keep your eye out for bears."

Said the man confidently walking off with our only gun.

He made his way down the steep slope and headed off on the trail to the outhouse.

"One for the pancakes, one for me," I said to myself, as I alternated plopping blueberries into my bowl and mouth. "One for the pancakes, two for me. One for the pancakes, three for me…"

Barely ten blueberry minutes later…

"One for the pancakes…I'm full. Two for the pancakes…I don't even want pancakes anymore."

Suddenly, there was a crashing sound from the bushes above me, accompanied by a drawn-out growl. From the sound of it, a bear was thundering through the brush and heading straight for me!

I stood up a little too quickly, and my left leg went out from under me. The next thing I knew, I was tumbling down the hill. I did my own version of "stop, drop, and roll," only it was "stop, drop, and roll, roll, roll, roll…"

I held on valiantly to my bowl, blueberries flying in all directions, as I flipped over and over and over. I didn't stop rolling until I hit the trail, covered in blueberry stains and nettles. I was trying to scramble to my feet when I heard hysterical laughter coming from the top of the hill. At first I thought I was being mocked by a bear. Then I realized it was Rob.

Furious, I threw the bowl straight at him, but it landed three feet to my right. I'm not good at sports.

When coming back from the outhouse, Rob had decided to play a practical joke. He climbed up the back of the hill and came at me from above, smashing through the trees and growling like a bear. His plan had worked flawlessly, and now I was the one growling in anger and in need of an outhouse.

This was going to call for some strategically plotted revenge. But I had to wait for just the right opportunity, which didn't present itself until an entire year later, when we were back at the gold mine—and when he was least expecting it.

Rob had decided he needed to cut down a dead tree near the mining site before it toppled over on its own accord and landed on our car, Rob, or worse yet, me. This tree grew on the side of a hill. It was downhill from our only road, but it shot up so high that its top loomed over it. Rob's plan was to cut off the dead tree at its base. When the tree fell, the top would come crashing down across the road.

"Head back to the cabin," Rob warned, knowing I was an expert at getting hurt. "I don't want you anywhere near where the tree lands."

Rob was treating me like a total idiot. Did he really think I wouldn't be able to see a huge tree falling? Avoiding it would be a piece of cake. *Mmmm, cake*, I thought, contemplating the taste of chocolate icing, the moist texture of the dessert, running my fork through...

"Torry!" Rob shouted. "Move!"

"All right, all right."

I hustled down the road a ways while Rob headed down the steep embankment, disappearing completely. The chain saw roared to life as he began to cut the base of the tree. That's when I remembered that I still owed him for the blueberry incident. I turned around and headed back up the road, creeping as close as I could to where I thought the tree would land without hitting me.

The tree finally came crashing down, landing directly on the spot where Rob said it would. *This is my chance!* Rob was still below the road, so I was completely out of view. Running up to the fallen tree, I crouched down and scooted safely beneath the heavy treetop. Then I threw my arms out to the side, closed my eyes, and let my mouth drop open in dramatic fashion. I'm always looking for opportunities to flex my acting muscles, and I knew how to play dead better than any possum.

I lay there, eyes closed, trying to keep my breathing light so he couldn't see the rise and fall of my chest. I heard his footsteps running toward me.

"Torry! Torry!"

Rob stood above me in a full-blown panic, and as he reached down to lift the tree off of me, I popped open my eyes.

"You forgot to say 'Timber,'" I said.

When I started laughing, Rob could have killed me. In fact, he picked up the top of the tree and slammed it back down on me. Once. Twice. Three times. After assaulting me with a deadly evergreen, he stormed off, not even bothering to help me up.

I tried to defend my actions by shouting after him, "Remember the blueberries?" But I think he had so much steam coming out of his ears that he couldn't hear me.

* * * * * * * * *

Death and danger lurk everywhere in the wild, so it's beyond me why Rob and I went to great lengths to fabricate phony fears—like attacking bears or deadly falling trees. I suppose humor is one way we deal with our anxieties.

However, when anxiety becomes an obstacle in the pursuit of our calling, it's no laughing matter—especially when our fears are phony. Most of them exist only in our heads, after all. The fear of failing, the fear of rejection, and sometimes even the fear of success...They all stand in the path of our calling, like enormous dead trees.

That's why I like to think of God as a divine Lumberjack sharpening up His ax to clear out all of the dead wood in my life—although for me, He's going to need a chain saw and a backhoe. And for my problems with deep roots...He's going to need a bulldozer.

8
OF MICE AND MEN

My dad was a fan of all sorts of wildlife, trying to make pets out of everything from skunks to raccoons. But there was one animal he had no tolerance for—mice. In our cabin, mice swarmed everywhere. You would see a group of them scurry when you turned on the lantern. They would often nibble at the bottom of my sleeping bag while I was sleeping, and they would come out of nowhere when you least expected it.

Once, Mom had cooked up stew, and as was the custom, she and my dad had invited over about a dozen other miners, young and old.

My mom served her friend Susan, dishing some stew into her bowl. Susan was about to sit down at the table when *SPLAT!* Something cannonballed from the ceiling and landed right in the stew. Then *SPLAT!* Another brown something crash-landed on the chair where she was about to sit.

All eyes stared at the two things sprawled out before them. Then they looked up to see a mouse nest in the cabin rafters. Two poor baby mice had tumbled out of the nest and fallen to their deaths. I wonder to this day if the mice had been showering too close to the edge of the nest, like me by the back door of our cabin. Or maybe they were the Three Blind Mice and one just hadn't dropped yet.

At first my mom thought for sure that my dad had pulled a prank on everyone. He had a greater reputation for practical jokes than even Rob or me. But this was no joke. Two mice had done swan dives from the ceiling.

That was the last straw for my dad, and he was determined to do something.

To take care of the mouse problem, my dad recruited the services of a cat named Killer. I remember when he first put the cat down in the middle of the kitchen floor. We all sat and watched, waiting for Killer to claim its first in a long line of victims. We stared in suspense as if we were watching a nature show involving a lion and a gazelle.

Decades later we're still waiting.

What was wrong with this cat? Was it a vegetarian? Opposed to capital punishment? He just lay around watching mice roam freely throughout the cabin. He barely even moved! And that's when I realized—he was union.

One time Rob was so disgusted with the cat's lack of motivation that he laid out a mousetrap and added peanut butter as bait. He had a mouse within an hour. Rob removed the mouse, set aside the trap, and placed the tiny corpse right in front of the cat's eyes to see if he showed even the slightest bit of interest. Killer stood up. He stared long and hard at the rodent. We held our breath in anticipation as he approached the mouse—and then gingerly stepped over it to eat the peanut butter.

This cat made Garfield look like an overachiever. It even appeared on *Cat* magazine's "Least Influential Cats of the Century" list.

In fact, it turned out that our *cabin* did a better job of killing mice than the cat.

When Rob and I showed up at the cabin one weekend to do some mining, we noticed the oddest thing. Inside the cabin, above the door frame, we spotted the back end of a mouse sticking out from a narrow crack. Somehow the house had settled at the exact moment that this mouse was trying to squeeze through the crack. Talk about bad timing. The settling of the house trapped and killed the poor mouse, leaving its tail and hindquarters sticking out of the wall like the shoes of the Wicked Witch sticking out from under Dorothy's house in *The Wizard of Oz*.

My dad had even posted a sign above the dead mouse: HOUSE 1, CAT 0.

● ● ● ● ● ● ● ● ●

Just as our cat forgot how to be a cat, we often forget what we're created for. We're constantly looking for the next step in our lives. We want God to give us direction, to show us what He wants from us, when He has already told us what He wants: "We are God's handiwork, created in Christ Jesus to do good works, which God prepared in advance for us to do" (Ephesians 2:10).

Do you want to know what God has called you to do? Love God. Love others. Serve the poor. Worship Him. Give freely. Make disciples. Do what God has prepared in advance for you to do, and the other stuff will come too.

I'm thankful that Jesus never forgot the reason He came. In Mark 10:45, Jesus said, "The Son of Man did not come to be served, but to serve, and to give his life as a ransom for many." He came to save us from death, save us from ourselves, and save us from our sins. Jesus came to save us from the terrible clutches of the devil himself. And in that remarkable moment when God boots Satan into the eternal abyss, I'm sure my dad will post a sign: GOD 1, SATAN 0.

9

MY HOMEBUOY

Rob is the person who led me to the Lord 20 years ago. He's my number one spiritual mentor, my best friend, and the person who keeps me accountable.

I think it's dangerous for a Christian man to live alone. It's hard to be accountable when there's no one to be accountable to. No one knows what you're watching online, no one knows who you bring into your home, no one knows what you do, and for me, that's an open door for all kinds of temptations. You need to take spiritual safety measures. Rob is mine, and I'm his. We have that in common. Other than that, we are complete polar opposites. For example:

He's intelligent. Me? Not so much.

He's thin. Me? Not so much.

He's focused. Me? How did I get barbecue sauce on my shirt? I didn't even eat...Wait, what were we talking about? Oh, yeah. The differences between Rob and me.

To illustrate, let's go back to a day we went to Walmart. For the first ten minutes of the drive, we rode in complete silence, as only good friends (or complete strangers) can comfortably do. I decided to start a conversation, but first I pressed Record on my phone because I sensed that something eloquent was going to come out of his mouth. What follows is a word-for-word transcript of that conversation.

TORRY: What are you thinking about?

ROB: A turbocharged two-cycle, direct-injected diesel engine with supplemental water injection.

TORRY (*reaching for Advil out of the glove box*): Aaand you were thinking that because…?

ROB: Well—I want to rebuild the carburetor on my weed eater, which uses a two-cycle engine, and I remembered reading in an article that direct-injection greatly increases fuel efficiency of two-cycle engines. Then I thought about my diesel tractor engine and what if you increased the compression and made a two-cycle diesel. Then I remembered another article I read where a guy added a separate injection of water to create steam instead of fuel on alternate cycles. Then I thought about the inherent problems normally aspirated two-cycles have, and I figured that adding a turbo would do the trick.

TORRY (*huge pause while taking another Advil*)

ROB: Why, what were you thinking about?

TORRY: Chocolate.

ROB (*pauses*): Why?

TORRY (*shrugs*): I like it.

On the surface, Rob may seem like the type of man who talks about engines with people he just met at the grocery store and later eats large amounts of meat without washing his hands. But he is also one of the most sensitive men I know.

One evening when we were living in Alaska, Rob and I were invited to our pastor's house for dinner. We never passed up a free meal, because we had no money in Alaska. But when we walked into Pastor Aiken's house, people jumped out of all sorts of hiding places, yelling, "Surprise!"

Rob had organized a surprise birthday party for me—the only one

I'd ever had. I was touched by the effort and truly surprised. But that was nothing compared to what came later.

Rob had bought and wrapped a present, and he handed it to me. It was a ream of paper.

"O...kay," I said. "Thanks?" *This will be great for keeping the fire going.*

"Wait, I've got something else for you too."

Ooooo, I hope it's a pencil!

It wasn't. It was a brand-new printer. *Okay. But you know this only works with...*

He brought out another package.

It was a computer—the first computer I ever owned. This was the best gift anyone had ever given me, not only because I knew how much money he spent on it (and how little of that he actually had) but also because he was showing he believed in me more than I believed in myself. *He actually thinks I can write!*

With tears in my eyes, I thanked him. He told me to shut up and cut the cake. He was hungry.

Rob is also my spiritual mentor. He not only tries to keep me walking in the right direction but also knocks me on the noggin when I'm headed in the wrong one. In addition, he encourages me to step out in faith, even when it means risking embarrassment. Like the time I traveled with Rob to Silver Dollar City, a Wild West theme park in Branson, Missouri.

"I think God wants me to write a humor column," I told Rob as we made the long drive west from Tennessee.

"So write a humor column."

"It's not that easy! You don't just write a humor column!"

"Whatever."

That wasn't helpful. I wanted him to give me confirmation or to talk me out of it, but he "Robbed" me of both. He didn't have the slightest idea what I was up against. Whenever I faced a blank page, writer's block loomed. My OCD would kick in, and I would obsess over every single word. So why in the world did I think God wanted me to write a regular column? I wasn't sure if I could pull it off unless "regular" meant once every five years.

In Branson we moseyed down the main street—well, actually Rob tried to mosey, but he doesn't have the hips for it. I was built for moseying.

We were approaching the log ride when I laid eyes on a woman sitting at a long folding table, eating a burrito. She'd set up right along the park's main drag, but the table didn't have anything else on it, which I thought was a bit odd. *Does she haul around a folding table wherever she goes, just so she'll have a place to eat whenever the fancy strikes?*

And then I had an even odder thought, but this time I gave voice to it.

"Rob, I feel like I'm supposed to go talk to that lady," I said.

"So go talk to her."

· "Robbed" again. I wanted to talk this through with him, and he was being so matter-of-fact.

"But what if I look stupid?"

"You should be used to it."

"*Rob!*"

"If you think God wants you to talk to someone, just go do it."

"But what if I'm wrong?"

"You won't learn how to distinguish your own voice from God's voice if you're not willing to embarrass yourself. Trust me, if you embarrass yourself enough times, you'll figure it out."

It was all so logical, but it still didn't make sense.

"Will you come with me?" I asked Rob.

He shook his head. "Nope. That's something God's calling *you* to do. God's calling *me* to go on the log ride."

So it was either gonna be the log ride or the lady for me. Knowing the log ride would frizz my hair, I chose the latter. Rob took off, leaving me to face the burrito lady all by myself. Steeling my nerves, I sauntered over, and the woman looked up and greeted me.

"Hi!" she exclaimed with a grin, revealing a piece of cilantro caught between her two front teeth. I couldn't take my eyes off of the big piece of greenery.

"Hi," I said. "Um...er...You've...uh...You've got a little something on your..."

I gestured to my own teeth.

"Oh!" she said cheerily. Then she lifted the cilantro from her front tooth with her tongue and drew it into her mouth like a lizard snagging a fly.

"Thanks!" she chirped.

I was confused. *Is that it, God? Is that all you wanted me to do—just tell this woman about the cilantro in her teeth? Gee, you really do care about the little things.*

I continued to stand there feeling awkward, uncertain of what to do or say next. Just then a man strode up carrying a cardboard box, and he began yanking out magazines and plopping them in a stack on the table.

"This is my husband, Philip, and I'm Amber," said the woman. "We're giving away free magazines today. Would you like one?"

"Sure," I said. I plucked a copy from the top of the stack and was surprised to see it was a Christian magazine for teens. Still feeling awkward and unsure whether my job here was done, I decided to stall for time. I opened the magazine to a random page and began to read. The article was pretty funny, and I chuckled to myself.

Amber looked up at me. "What?"

"Sorry, I'm just reading this. It's pretty funny."

She glanced at the story I was reading and said, "Oh yeah, that's our humor columnist. We just lost him, and I need to find a new one."

They lost their humor columnist?

Once again, in typical Torry fashion, the words started pouring out of me. I told Amber that I was a comedian and a writer for *Adventures in Odyssey*, and I'd be very interested in applying to write a humor column. She told me to write some samples and send them her way, and she'd check them out. And that's how I wound up writing a humor column for *On Course* magazine for 12 years.

After the magazine closed down, I kept writing for Amber when she moved to *Leading Hearts* magazine. I continue to write for them today, and thanks to Amber's excellent editing, I have won three Evangelical Press Association Awards for the column. That's a strange thing to come from a spontaneous conversation with a stranger. But in truth, it wasn't spontaneous. It was a divine appointment, and it took Rob to urge me to risk embarrassment and pursue it.

Proverbs 27:17 says, "As iron sharpens iron, so one person sharpens another." And that's what Rob does for me.

*   *   *   *   *   *   *   *   *

Following your God-given calling is like swimming in the ocean. (I'm more of a floater than a swimmer, but this is the only analogy I could think of that makes sense.) You can see the shore ahead, and you're desperately heading toward it. But the waves get high. You get tired. The shore is so far away, and you feel like you're not getting any closer. That's when you decide to forget it and stop swimming, and you either sink or let the tide take you farther away. That's also when you need a buoy—something to keep you afloat until you're ready to go for the shore again.

Rob is my spiritual flotation device—my homebuoy. I often feel sorry for him, being out there in the middle of the ocean with me, constantly having to keep my head above water while I flail about. But he is the one God gave me. He is often the reason I keep swimming.

"I'm drowning," I'd say.

"Then swim," he'd reply.

Robbed again.

PANNING FOR GOLD. When it comes to friends, Rob is the gold standard.

DUCK DYNASTY BODYGUARD. I'm thankful for a friend who always has my back.

10
SAUERKRAUT HEAVEN

randma never did anything wrong. And I know that because I was told by an authority on the subject—my grandma. Here is a case in point...

"Let's go through the drive-through!" she shouted one day as if she were Columbus discovering America.

I could hardly believe what I was hearing. Grandma Burmaster never trusted the bank drive-through, so this was a momentous occasion. She was of the generation that walked into the bank lobby, handed their money to a real person, and walked out with a receipt and a free sucker.

Grandma and I were late getting to the movie theater, so that's what led to her impulsive decision to use the drive-through for the very first time. As she pulled up, she confidently grabbed the pneumatic tube carrier and carefully set it aside. This confused me a little. But what confused me even more was when she placed her checks directly into the pneumatic system's door, and with a little extra gusto she pushed Send with her index finger.

"Grandma! No!" I shouted.

Too late. The checks, which were supposed to be placed in the tube carrier, were sucked into the system. It made a sound I'll never forget.

WOOOK-FRAGGLE-FRAGGLE-GAGGLE-GOB!

For those of you who cannot read sound effects, it was something between the sound of a shoelace getting caught in a vacuum cleaner and the sucking sound of a plunger. There may have been a little lip smacking at the end.

Suffice it to say, the checks did not reach the teller. They became stuck in limbo somewhere between the car and the bank. I despaired that we were going to miss the movie previews, and over the next ten excruciating minutes, Grandma and the bank teller negotiated the best way to retrieve the checks. The teller told her (I guess that's why he's called a teller) she should send the empty tube carrier through the system to dislodge the lost checks. So she did.

WOOOG-OOOM-BUBB-BUBB-BUBB-BWAGG!

The teller sent the tube back, Grandma fired it off to him again, he returned it to her—it was like they were playing Ping-Pong. The people in the cars lined up behind us were clearly annoyed by this game.

Finally, all of the checks made it through—mangled, torn at the corners, and streaked with black gunk. As Grandma drove off, she spun toward me and declared, "And *that's* why I never go through the drive-through!"

Clearly it was not her fault.

I loved my grandma, who passed away almost 20 years ago. As far as I was concerned, she was the best grandma a boy could ever have.

One day when I was eight years old, I was on my grandma's floor reading comic books while my mom, grandma, and aunt played cards nearby. Glancing up from my Superman comics, I was shocked to witness a crime taking place.

"Grandma, you already drew a card."

"No, I didn't."

"Yes, you did. I saw you!"

"You're imagining things."

"Why don't you count your cards just to make sure?"

Pretending to have just discovered her "mistake," she exclaimed, "Oh, h-e-double toothpicks!"

"I can s-p-e-double toothpicks, you know," I responded.

Ignoring me, she continued to excuse her mistake. "I wonder how that happened. Must be old age." Then she shot me a dirty look. "And if you want to live to an old age, you'll hush up and read your comics."

In another incident, my father was working the checkout counter at the local grocery store when he looked outside, and there was Grandma Burmaster parking sideways in the lot, taking up *three* desirable spots right in front of the store. As she entered the store and passed the checkout line, my dad pointed out her parking problem, and she snapped over her shoulder, "I'm parked exactly where I want to be!"

If Jesus had told her, "You're a sinner," she would've probably blamed old age and taken up three parking places right outside the pearly gates.

Grandma was my friend, my confidant, and someone who was sincerely and enthusiastically interested in everything I did. Her full name was Ulily Mae Burmaster, but no one dared call her Ulily. She hated the name just as much as I hated the "De" in Torry De Martin. If she ever called me Torry De, I was quick to answer, "Yes, Ulily Mae?" (But only if I was out of slapping range. I was disrespectful but not stupid.)

A compassionate soul, Grandma spent many years working at a nursing home. She was pained to see how many of the residents seldom had any visitors, so she'd send me to the rooms of residents who she knew were particularly lonely.

"Ask Eunice in room 202 to tell you about her favorite horse growing up," she'd encourage me. "Go visit Frank in 205 and ask him to tell you one of his World War II stories."

Grandma was a loving person, but she wasn't a Christian when I was a boy, in part because it's sometimes hard for "good people" to come to the Lord. She was raised in a good home and didn't commit any of the "big sins," and it's difficult for such people to accept the need for redemption.

Another reason might be that she had a hard time admitting when she was wrong—a key step in accepting salvation.

My grandma was a rascal, and I loved her to pieces. I was devastated a few years after I moved to Alaska when I heard that she had lung cancer. She battled it for five years, but the final year was the worst because that's when the cancer struck with a vengeance.

That year I traveled to the Christian Artists Seminar in the Rockies, and I planned a three-day layover in Seattle to visit Grandma on the way back to Alaska. My mom picked me up at the Seattle airport, but I was stunned to see Rob was with her. Unbeknownst to me, Rob had impulsively booked the trip from Alaska to Washington to surprise me. As it turned out, he was as excited as I was about the awards I won at the conference and couldn't wait the three days to celebrate with me. He also wanted to join me in saying good-bye to my grandma—the same grandma who had played the infamous Christmas ornament prank on him when he first met our family. (Check it out in *Of Moose and Men*.)

When I saw Grandma, she had lost a lot of weight. She wasn't as lively and joy-filled, because the cancer had sucked the energy out of her. Since I was living in Alaska, where I couldn't see my grandmother, I had been in denial about her looming death. But when I saw Grandma's face, there was no running away from the reality of the hold that cancer had on her. I didn't have the money to travel from Alaska to Washington very often, so I knew this would probably be the last time I saw her.

Although she looked frail, her face softened as the disease progressed. This feisty old woman was actually beginning to look more angelic than ever. Of course, she had always looked angelic to me, in part because she was surrounded by clouds of her own cigarette smoke, which sometimes formed a halo over her head.

Each conversation felt like the last. My heart was continually breaking.

I said my good-byes to Grandma and then headed back to Alaska, worried about her eternity. This led me to the Christian bookstore, where I hoped to find something that might speak to her, and I discovered a book by Joni Eareckson Tada—*Heaven: Your Real Home*. When I read the book in my Alaskan cabin, I loved it. Joni described heaven as an amazing place with no more pain and sickness. The old image of angels sitting around playing harps makes heaven sound as boring as h-e-double toothpicks, but Joni made heaven seem so beautiful and exciting that you wanted to go there right away.

Joni's book comforted me, but I couldn't help thinking about how much it might also comfort Grandma. My grandma didn't have the energy to read anymore, so I bought the audiobook and sent it to my mom, who played it for her.

Grandma was so intrigued and comforted by listening to the book that she started asking to hear it every day. One afternoon after Grandma had listened to the audiobook once again, my mom asked if she would like to turn her life over to Jesus, and Grandma said very simply and clearly, "Yes." She said it with the same level of confidence as when she said, "I'm parked exactly where I want to be." Only this time she was saying, "I'm going exactly where I want to go."

At long last, Grandma responded to the Lion's roar. She set aside her stubbornness and answered the ultimate call in her life. The call to surrender. I will never forget hearing my mom tell me about Grandma's decision, because I had been so worried about sending that audiobook. How do you share your faith with your own beloved grandmother? She was always the one who taught me, not the other way around.

I will always be grateful for that book and how it changed Grandma's life. That's why I was thrilled when I had a chance to share my thanks to Joni in person in 2000. Strolling down the hall at the National Religious Broadcasters convention, I was shocked to see Joni waiting to get on an elevator with her assistant. Joni was in a wheel-chair, due to a tragic accident in 1967 when she dove into shallow water in Chesapeake Bay, fractured her spine, and became paralyzed from the shoulders down.

Joni was a celebrity, so I knew that as soon as other people spotted her, she was going to be swarmed. I didn't have much time, so in typical Torry fashion, I bypassed the small talk and blurted out the "big talk." I quickly explained how her book had changed my grandmother's eternity, and I could tell by her expression that she was moved by my grandma's story. To her, I wasn't just a face in the crowd, just another admirer. Joni was genuinely interested, and she asked if I could write down my grandma's story and send it to her. But every time I tried, I'd get too emotional. I'm doing it now, 17 years later. Better late than never.

Thank you, Joni.

You know, I think one reason the book had such an influence on Grandma was that she was hearing about heaven from Joni—someone who knew what it was like to suffer. As my grandma learned during that tough final year, life can be painful. In fact, it can be a lot like making sauerkraut.

One of my favorite family traditions was making sauerkraut at Grandma's house. More than 20 of us would pack into Grandma's kitchen, where we dumped out five or six boxes of cabbage heads and began the magical process of transforming them into sauerkraut.

We'd strip off the outer leaves, cut the cabbage into quarters, remove the hearts, and use a kraut cutter (yes, there is such a thing) to slice them up. Next, we sprinkled the cabbage with canning salt and stuffed the concoction into our crocks. Then came the most important part. Using a baseball bat with a round piece of wood attached to the end, the kids would pound down on the cabbage mixture, causing that all-important juice to squeeze out. It was a tough, smelly job, but we were promised homemade ice cream when we finished, so we worked our tails off—although after partaking of so much ice cream, I got my tail back pretty quickly.

Once we finished pounding the mixture in the crocks, we placed a plate and a gallon of water on top of each cabbage concoction. This applied pressure over the next few weeks, producing those good juices and slowly transforming the cabbage into delectable sauerkraut.

(And if you're one of those people who don't think sauerkraut is delectable, I'll pray that your sanity is restored.)

Sometimes the trials of our "sauerkraut life" make us want to exclaim, "What a crock!" This is especially true when we feel the intense pressures of life—a persistent pounding that beats us down. Some people allow this pressure to destroy them, but God often uses it to produce those "good juices." The best result is when we allow the pressure to change us and turn us into something that is beautiful, useful, and delectable (to sane people).

We stored our sauerkraut out in the pump house until it was ready to can. Then, on New Year's Eve, our family's tradition was for all of us to take our first bite of the sauerkraut at midnight. We'd haul out the jars, jab in our forks, and take our first bites while laughing, telling stories, and hoping and praying for a prosperous new year. Heaven will be like that—fellowship, fun, and food. Every moment in heaven will feel like a New Year's celebration—fresh and filled with promise, spilling over with hope.

That last year was rough on Grandma, and for a time she must have felt like one of those mangled checks in the pneumatic tube. But she made it through to the other side, and I look forward to someday reuniting with her in heaven, where I can read comics on her dining room floor and smell the scent of her fresh-baked cookies for eternity.

Then, when all is said and done, we'll open a fresh jar of sauerkraut, dip in our forks, share a bite, and together we'll watch Joni Eareckson Tada dance.

SAYING GOODBYE. This is the last photo taken of Rob and me
with my beloved Grandma Burmaster.

DIVINE APPOINTMENT. I took this photo with Joni Eareckson
Tada at the NRB Convention after stopping her at the elevator
to tell her about my grandma.

11
HUGGIES

What's this?" Rob asked, pointing to a piece of paper on the fridge.

"The dog hugging schedule," I said.

He sighed and shook his head. Clearly this was going to be a long story. "A what?"

I told him I'd just read about a University of North Carolina study that found that hugs have health benefits. Hugs "increased levels of oxytocin, a 'bonding' hormone, and reduced blood pressure—which cuts the risk of heart disease," reported BBC News. In this study, 38 couples were asked to hug for 20 seconds three times a day, and they were found to have significantly higher levels of oxytocin afterward.

If oxytocin helps humans live longer, it's gotta apply to dogs too, I thought. *This is a pet emergency! If humans need three 20-second hugs a day, and one human year equals seven dog years, how many times do I need to hug my dogs a day? Okay, I'm gonna need to do the hug math.*

Four hours later, I had concluded that I should multiply three hugs per day times seven, which meant I should hug each dog 21 times every day.

Then I remembered that because dogs mature faster, the first year of a dog's life equals 15 human years. For puppies, my final calculation was 45 hugs per day during their first year of life. Two hours after that, I realized my dogs weren't puppies anymore, so it didn't even apply.

But what about our cats? Don't they deserve hugs too? I discovered that after the age of two, cats age four human years every year. That means my cats should get 12 hugs per day. But hold on! Rain and Rocky are outdoor cats, and they age twice as fast as indoor cats, so they get 24 hugs each day. Also, cats have nine lives, so does that mean...? Oh, I give up. That's too much math. Besides, cats spend most of their time licking their fur. They can take care of themselves.

I had all of this plotted out on paper when Rob came home and saw the sheet on the refrigerator. Fortunately, he didn't see the other 27 wadded-up sheets I used to calculate this.

"I'm serious," I said. "We're gonna need to divvy it up. I'll do from eight to five when you're at work, but you're on call from five to twelve when I write."

Rob pulled the sheet down from the refrigerator and said, "I think we better replace this with a business card for a therapist."

"But Rob..."

"Three hugs are enough. You can't give up your career to hug dogs."

As Rob crumpled up the paper, I exclaimed, "Hey! Don't throw that away! It took me all day to figure that out. I even broke your calculator." (I had thrown it in frustration.)

However, Rob refused even to consider following a dog hug schedule.

"Okay, fine," I said. "Go ahead and let the dogs be oxytocin deprived, but I'm not robbing myself of it. Give me a hug."

Rob paused a moment, flattened out the paper, and put it back on the fridge. "Which dog do you want first?"

* * * * * * * * *

The upshot is that I try to hug my dogs regularly each day, accounting for 21 minutes of hugging and 28 minutes with my lint brush afterward. But even more importantly, I try to maintain the same regular connection with God. I'll fire off quick prayers to Him throughout the day, and I'm sure God feels the same way we feel when we get hugs from spouses or nuzzles from pets. He feels joy when we lean against Him and relax and accept His love.

For the life of me, I don't know how people can get through a single day without prayer, without connecting to the Lord. How do they get by without feeling the warmth of God's embrace? It doesn't take long to send short prayers to your Father, even during the busiest of days.

Prayer is far better than an oxytocin release any day, and even in the darkest of times, He will embrace us with a holy hug that will last as long as we want. Far longer than 20 seconds.

You don't need to make a schedule to stick on your fridge though. He's available anytime.

HOW NOT TO HUG YOUR CAT. Don't try this at home. (Photo by Lucas Wilson)

12

FORSAKEN BACON

I was living in a remote cabin in Alaska 20 years ago when I first felt a calling to return to acting. Hollywood is a long way from Bear Valley, so it sounded impossible at the time. (You've got your work cut out with that one, God.) But now here I was on a movie set, actually standing next to...

Well, I'd better not say.

We were specifically told not to talk to this legendary actress on the set, so putting her name in print might not be a good idea. Let's just call her Famous Actress—although we could also call her High Maintenance Actress, since it took a major effort for the producers to find just the right hotel for her. She had to have just the right room facing just the right direction so the sunrise would cast its light in just the right spot every morning. It was like casting Goldilocks.

Famous Actress also had handlers swarming all over her. But there I was, standing alone with her between scenes. It seemed strange just to stand there and not say anything. It also seemed a little rude, but I knew the rule: We weren't supposed say a word to her, even if her pants were on fire.

Then again, who would know? It was just the two of us.

How could a few words—a tiny spark of human interaction—possibly hurt anything? As I contemplated whether I should risk speaking to her, my eyes wandered down to her left hand, and I saw that she wore a gorgeous—and colossal—wedding ring. It looked like four bands had been soldered together to create a staggered stairway of diamonds all around it.

My ADHD was so drawn to the sparkly object that my jaw dropped and the words spilled out.

"That's a beautiful ring."

"Oh thank you, darling," Famous Actress said while extending her hand to give me a closer look. "The first three rings are from my first three husbands, and I had my fourth husband connect them all together. The biggest diamond is from him." She paused before adding, "But he didn't last long."

She said it like it was the most natural thing in the world, but I couldn't help thinking, *You had your fourth husband weld together the wedding rings from your first three husbands? That marriage was doomed from the start!*

Fortunately, I didn't voice these thoughts. Even I wasn't dumb enough to make such an observation out loud. I breathed a sigh of relief. I had successfully completed a conversation with Famous Actress without embarrassing myself. It was something I could use as a conversation starter for the rest of my life. *I should just shut up now, and everything will be perfect.*

Nope. Not happening.

"Wow," I said with a chuckle, "if you get married a few more times, you'll have yourself a nice set of brass knuckles."

Then I laughed at my own joke to show I was kidding.

Dead silence. I think the room temperature dropped 30 degrees in one second. Somehow, someway, I had managed to stick my entire foot into my mouth all the way up to my knee.

I felt like a brass knucklehead.

I'd really love to tell you who this woman was, but I can't. She may have had four husbands, but she has 11 lawyers.

One year later, I was performing at a conference called "A Time to

Hope, a Time to Heal," run by a good friend of mine named Fatima. The conference focused on women who were struggling in the aftermath of an abortion. I was the only male speaker, and while I didn't know anything about counseling women who had abortions, I did know a lot about living with regrets. I share my own stories, sprinkled heavily with humor, and my job was to offer comic relief in the midst of a very difficult topic.

I walked into the green room and spotted another famous actress (not the one with the rings). Since we're friends now, I can mention her name—the incredibly talented and beautiful Jennifer O'Neill, who has appeared in over 35 feature movies, including the one that made her a star, *The Summer of '42*. She was a model and spokesperson for CoverGirl and is an advocate for many charitable organizations, such as World Vision and the American Cancer Society.

Most importantly though, Jennifer is a strong Christian and wonderful woman.

Whenever I'm around prominent people, something happens to me. My social anxiety swings into full gear, which leads to stumbling and clumsiness, like the time I was performing at a Microsoft party and spilled Coke on Bill Gates. Trying to cover up my faux pas, I attempted my best James Bond imitation while introducing myself. "Martin. Torry Martin. I have a license to spill."

Gates didn't laugh, so I changed the subject. "Have you seen the hors d'oeuvres guy?"

"No," he said, while dabbing his shirt. "But if I do, I'll warn him you're coming."

With Jennifer O'Neill, I sensed that my foot was already starting to make travel plans to visit my mouth, so I made a mental note: *Don't say anything stupid.*

Jennifer introduced me to her friends, a pastor and his wife, in the green room. "I saw the movie you did with [Famous Actress]," the pastor's wife said. "What was it like to work with her?"

What a great conversation starter! It allowed me to tell a story about putting my foot in my mouth—without saying anything stupid. I proceeded to tell them the story about the Famous Actress and her four wedding bands. However, when I got to the brass knuckles punch line, nobody laughed except me. Awkward silence.

After the three of them excused themselves, I shared with my friend Fatima the story I told and how nobody laughed.

"Umm... Torry, I don't know if you realize this, but Jennifer O'Neill has been married nine times."

I was horrified. *No wonder no one laughed! I'm such an idiot.* I guess the lesson here is, never make a joke about a woman who has been married four times in front of a woman who has been married nine times.

Jennifer O'Neill (who, by the way, has now been married to the same man for more than 20 years) is very honest about her many marriages and struggles in her life. That's why she was the main speaker at the "A Time to Hope, a Time to Heal" conference. In her twenties, Jennifer gave in to pressure from her fiancé to get an abortion. It led to tremendous regret and guilt, and she believes it contributed to nine miscarriages.

"We're told it's nothing," she once said about abortion, "but it's everything."

Jennifer was at the conference to offer hope to women who might be going through the same struggles, and I had no excuse for my blunder. When famous actresses see me coming, they should realize that it's a Time to Hope that I don't talk to them, a Time to Heal if I do, and a Time to Run if they spot me first!

I thought it was brave for Jennifer to be so open in sharing her story, and she has inspired me to be just as vulnerable in telling mine. Jesus has a knack for redeeming our past, present, and future in unpredictable ways. When God challenged me to leave my cabin in Alaska to pursue my calling, the biggest obstacle was that I didn't think the Lord could use me because of my past. But Jesus invites us to remove the shackles of our past and be restored for His purposes. If only we could see ourselves—and other people—the way that Jesus does.

Once upon a time, when I was reading *The Three Little Pigs* and

Little Red Riding Hood to my niece, she noticed that the Big Bad Wolf played a big role in both stories. And I'll never forget what my niece said: "Uncle Torry, why don't the Big Bad Wolf just get *saved*?"

What a great question! I thought. *Why doesn't he get saved? And what would happen if he did?*

My creative mind immediately kicked in at the mere suggestion of such a preposterous idea. I realized that I could use the Big Bad Wolf in a story to address any sin without being sin-specific. Everyone has a Big Bad Wolf sin—a sin that they think is worse than others. Even if the sin is in our past, we're still uncomfortable with it. I'm talking about drugs, hating sauerkraut, adultery, left-handedness, homosexuality, vegetarianism—you know, the *biggies*.

So I wrote a comedy sketch about what might happen if the Big Bad Wolf did become saved. Would Little Red Riding Hood be willing to forgive the Wolf for her past therapy expenses due to his grandmother-impersonation gig? Would the Three Little Pigs forgive him for their inflated insurance premiums due to his destruction of their homes?

In my retelling, Little Red Riding Hood did indeed offer forgiveness to the Wolf. But the Three Little Pigs refused to offer grace. "Not by the hair of our chinny, chin, chin!" they exclaimed in unison.

The Three Little Pigs were owners of a housing conglomerate, and although they were fine with the Big Bad Wolf repenting, they were not so fine with him attending their church.

"Who cares if he changed his name to the Big Blessed Wolf! We still don't want someone like *him* in our church," said one of the pigs.

The pigs—Peter, Paul, and Mary (named after the singers, not the biblical characters)—were the church's biggest tithers, so they threatened the pastor with a warning.

"We're the ones responsible for financing the church building project," Peter Pig told the pastor.

"Thanks to us," said Mary Pig, "the church is made of brick—not out of sticks or straw, which the church committee recommended to save money."

"If you let the Big Bad Wolf become a member here, just keep in mind…you'll lose us," said Paul Pig. "And our tithes."

The Three Little Pigs fully expected their pastor to crumble under their threats like a building made of straw. But the pastor was made of even sterner stuff than the bricks in the church walls. Instead of backing down, Parson Brown rose up.

"I'm sorry you guys feel that way, but please know that the door to this church will always be open to you if you decide to come back," he said. "But don't let it hit you in the ham hock on your way out."

The pigs were aghast as Parson Brown continued. "If we don't forgive others, how can we expect God to forgive us? God's Word says that if we forsake others, we risk being forsaken ourselves."

Outraged, the Three Little Pigs stormed from the church in a huff and a puff, preferring to wallow in their unforgiveness, like wallowing in mud. Forgiveness was just too hard, so they took their tithes somewhere else, and that is how they lived up to the title of my comedy sketch, "Forsaken Bacon."

Accepting grace for the Big Bad Wolf in my life is a hard lesson I've had to learn over and over again. The enemy's job is to get us to keep dredging up our past because he knows that our past sins can interfere with our present calling. He wants to blind us to the reality that God has called all of us on a great mission today, despite all we have done yesterday.

"Therefore, if anyone is in Christ, the new creation has come: The old has gone, the new is here!" (2 Corinthians 5:17). We're new creations. That's the message of the "A Time to Hope, a Time to Heal" conference. That's the message of Jennifer O'Neill. And that's the message of the gospel. God will take the brass knuckles in our lives—the source of so much pain and fighting—and He'll craft them into a beautiful wedding ring.

Or, in other words, God will save our bacon.

13

CENSOR AND SENSIBILITY

As an actor, I don't get called to as many auditions as I'd like because my appearance usually works against me. When casting directors are looking to cast a role, they have to go through hundreds of actor photos, searching for someone who is close to what they already envision a character to look like. Unless they're casting a human orangutan, my face won't be the first one they think of.

The only way to get around this dilemma is to find some actual face time with the casting director, with the hopes that personal interaction will cause him or her to look at you differently. Such meetings are few and far between. So when I heard that respected casting director Mark Fincannon would be speaking at a Faith in Film breakfast meeting in Atlanta, I knew I had to take advantage of the opportunity.

The night before I was to leave, I opened my desk drawer to look for my business cards. My eyes fell on a CD of my personal testimony, which I'd given at a conference, and I had an odd thought. *I should take that with me and give it to Mark Fincannon.*

Then I thought better of it. *No, I shouldn't. That'd be stupid.*

And so began the Battle of Torry's Brain.

TORRY 1: Just take it.

TORRY 2: That doesn't make sense. I want to look like a professional, not a proselytizer.

TORRY 1: What can it hurt?

TORRY 2: My career.

TORRY 1: What career?

TORRY 2: That's my point. I'm trying to get one.

TORRY 1: Take it!

TORRY 2: It'll feel awkward!

TORRY 1: You might regret it if you don't.

TORRY 2: Fine, I've got it. (*Slams the drawer*) Now shut up. (*Opens it again*) I forgot my business cards.

TORRY 1: You're so lucky you have me.

Mark Fincannon is an Emmy-winning, Hollywood casting director. The guy has over 170 credits, including some pretty big-name movies, including *The Blind Side*, *Ray*, and *The Patriot*. Why would he want to listen to a 90-minute testimony from some no-name actor? Giving him this CD made absolutely no sense to me.

The next morning, I dragged myself out of bed at three o'clock to jump on the road and drive three hours to Atlanta. But I was about ten miles from home when I realized I had forgotten to bring the CD, triggering the Battle of Torry's Brain II (the sequel):

TORRY 1: You forgot the CD.

TORRY 2: It's too late. Going back'll put us 20 minutes behind.

TORRY 1: You might regret it.

TORRY 2: It's three in the morning! Shut up!

TORRY 1: You also forgot your breakfast bar.

TORRY 2: Good point. (*U-turn*)

The Faith and Film breakfast was held in a studio, and when I arrived for the social time before Fincannon's talk, I hoped to catch a moment with the casting director.

But when I got there it looked hopeless.

Mark Fincannon was already surrounded by at least 20 very skinny and attractive actors and actresses. All of them were eager to get a foot in the door with Mark, and I wasn't any different—except for the skinny part. I couldn't very well shove my way through the crowd, knocking actors aside like a football lineman from *The Blind Side*— although my dad would've been proud that Touchdown Martin was finally showing some athletic prowess.

Looking on the bright side, I thought maybe the mob of actors and actresses keeping me from Mark Fincannon were doing me a favor. With my penchant for saying stupid things to prominent people, perhaps it was best if I couldn't get within shouting distance of him.

When Fincannon gave his talk, I was surprised because I was expecting to hear some advice on preparing for a role or something. But he ended up taking the entire time to share his personal testimony, and the stories he told of how God worked in his life were thrilling.

Hmm. Maybe giving him my testimony isn't so nuts.

That was when I realized I had left the audio CD back in my car. Do I run out and get the CD, knowing that the time I spent outside would be time that other people would be crowding him? Or do I go up to him now, forgoing the CD? By the time I decided, it was too late. He was swarmed again.

I was just getting ready to give up and leave when a screenwriter friend of mine, Cheryl, nabbed me and said, "Torry, I want you to come over and meet someone!"

"Sure," I said, following her.

Cheryl then introduced me to a lady named Sharon, and we had the most wonderful talk. I immediately sensed she was a kindred spirit, and we connected on a spiritual level.

Things were winding down when Sharon said, "My husband, Mark, just gave me the signal that we need to get going."

Mark?

At first the name didn't register. But then I noticed Sharon signaling back to her husband, and I was flabbergasted. *Her husband is Mark Fincannon!*

I'm glad that I didn't know who Sharon was. If I had, I would've tried too hard and said something stupid. With my penchant for saying the wrong thing, I could've ended my career in one fell swoop. Not knowing who she was, however, allowed me to be myself.

Suddenly, the battling Torrys were back.

TORRY 1: Go get the CD. Now!

TORRY 2: I'm going, I'm going!

TORRY 1: Come on, Tortoise, run!

TORRY 2: Don't call me that! And this *is* running!

TORRY 1: Really?

TORRY 2: Shut up.

I rushed out to my car and returned just in time to deliver the CD to Sharon. And by the way, handing it to her was just as awkward as I thought it would be. *Yeesh.*

TORRY 1: Good job, Torry 2!

TORRY 2: Yeah, thanks…for helping me seal my doom.

Two hours into my drive home, I got a phone call from Cheryl.

"Sharon just called and asked for your number. I wanted to make sure it was okay to give it to her," Cheryl said.

"Give it to *Sharon Fincannon*? Of course!" I exclaimed. "You can give her my phone number, address, email…You can even give her my credit card number, but only my Visa. That one's already maxed."

A few anxious days later, Sharon called me to say, "Mark and I listened to your testimony, and I just wanted to tell you how much we enjoyed it."

We must have talked for at least 30 minutes, but not once did the conversation ever go to anything professional. Instead, we talked entirely about spiritual matters. It was surprising and refreshing, and I was thankful for it.

I was even more surprised when she called back a week later.

"I don't know why I'm doing this," Sharon said, "but I felt led to call and tell you a story."

She shared with me that more than a year earlier, she and Mark had gone to a hospital to pray for a man who was terminally ill. The man's family was ready to take him off of life support, but Sharon felt compelled to tell the wife that a healing would take place. The last thing you want to do in such a tragic situation is give false hope to somebody, but Sharon said the sense was strong. So she boldly told the wife that the battle wasn't over yet. That was a risky thing for Sharon to say, and to everyone but Sharon's surprise, the man was healed.

"Anyway, that's it. I don't know why I was supposed to call and tell you that story, or even what it means," she told me. "I just felt that you would need it sometime in the future. Look, I've got to run, so we'll talk again soon! Okay?"

The whole call lasted less than two minutes.

That's weird, I thought. Based on that very brief phone call, Sharon sounded a little cray-cray. But I mentally rebuked myself for these thoughts.

In my Christian walk, I have discovered that there are "God sensors" and "God censors." A God censor puts limitations on God by saying, "Sorry, the Lord doesn't work that way." But a God sensor *senses* God and is always trying to discern what the Spirit is telling them, even if it makes them uncomfortable.

Clearly Sharon was a God sensor. When I thought she was crazy, I was acting like a God censor.

I was still baffled how Sharon's story could apply to me. But the more I thought about it, I realized there was a possibility that this could be a word from God, and to be honest it struck a little fear in me. What did it mean? Is something bad going to happen to a person close to me? I'm a chronic worrier anyway. *Do we have enough milk?*

Did Glenn from The Walking Dead *really die? Is McDonald's bringing back the McRib, or what?*

Not to mention I was about to leave for a conference to give a keynote address titled "The Shark Ate My Ichthus"—all about maintaining your character in the cutthroat world of the Christian entertainment industry. Christian entertainers were my audience, and I was worried about how it was going to go over with them. My fear wasn't just that the sharks in this industry would be annoyed with me; it was that they would no longer want to be in the same water with me. Who wants to work with the kid who peed in their pool?

I was afraid of falling flat on my face during my keynote, but falling facedown almost happened to me before I could even get out my door and on the road. I nearly tripped over the hulking animal that blocked my exit. A dog the size of a moose lay in front of our door, and he wouldn't move. He didn't have the energy.

Our dog Moose had been with us for nine years, entering our lives when Rob picked him out from a book of photos at PetSmart— kind of like a casting call audition, come to think of it. After seeing the photo, we drove out to a woman's house to take a look at him in person. But first I wrote a prayer on a sticky note and shoved it in my pocket: "Father, if there is a dog out there You want us to get, let somebody call that dog Moose—somebody other than me."

I shared the note with Rob and said, "Our new dog is going to be named Moose." But when Rob and I laid eyes on this goofy, gangly dog, we were sure he *wasn't* the right choice. When he trotted into the room, his tail was wagging so furiously that he whacked a cup off a coffee table. Then he turned around to see what the noise was and knocked over a pile of magazines. The dog was big and clumsy, and I envisioned him walking through our house with a trail of broken lamps lying in his wake. *You just keep right on walking.*

Wiping away the slobber that the dog had just drooled on my leg, I looked at Rob, and we agreed to pass. I was judging this dog from outward appearances, the same way people often judge me. But we were just leaving the woman's house when the animal shelter lady (who showed up as we were walking out) said, "I don't know why I'm saying this, but this dog is going to be a moose."

Rob dropped his head and rolled his eyes. "We'll take him," he mumbled.

We took the dog home, wrung out our slobber-covered clothes, and named our new mutt Moose. We also very quickly discovered why God had chosen him for us. Moose was a big dog with a big heart—a heart as big as an actual moose. He may be clumsy, but he was also the kindest and loyalest of dogs, and he immediately bonded with our other dog, Bear. Moose was Rob's dog, and Rob's affection came from Moose, while my affection came more from Bear and Willow.

Moose was a Fila Brasileiro, also known as a Brazilian mastiff. These dogs are bred to run, and they are used to cover thousands of acres on cattle ranches in Brazil. They tend to bond with one person and are highly protective. They are also incredibly faithful, which is why the Brazilians have an expression, "As faithful as a Fila."

Rob works for a security company, and he is often called out at night to repair ATM machines at banks. It can be a dangerous job. Two other employees in different parts of the country had been tricked into making middle-of-the-night repair calls to ATM machines and had been shot and killed during the ensuing robbery. That's why repairmen like Rob usually receive protection from guards when they go out in the middle of the night. But if the guards didn't get there in time, Rob always had Moose as a bodyguard backup.

It was Moose's nature to run, and sometimes he would disappear for hours. But amazingly he never wandered off when he made those late-night calls with Rob. He sat with his back to Rob, keeping a lookout, as if he knew there could be danger.

One night when Rob returned home from doing a service repair, Moose immediately took off running and disappeared for a spell. Rob was upset, but I had the perfect solution.

"If you want to keep Moose from running away, maybe you should put an ATM machine in the backyard," I told him.

Plus it'd be a lot more convenient for me, personal-banking wise.

But now, as I left for my conference, Moose's running days looked like they were nearing an end. Five months earlier, a tennis ball–sized tumor had been removed from his neck, and he also suffered through several months of chemotherapy. We thought he was doing well, but then...

Rob called me at the conference to give me the news I feared. "Moose has been passing a lot of blood."

After my keynote, I raced home a day early. And when I got there, it was bad. Moose, obviously in pain, could barely move, and it appeared we may have to put him down. Rob made an appointment with the vet for the following evening.

I saw that Rob's sleeping bag was in the middle of the floor where he had camped out next to Moose the night before. Rob and I lay down on either side of our buddy. We shed tears and prayed. I thanked God for giving us such a faithful canine companion, and then I pleaded between sobs, "Father, could we have just one more year with Moose? Just one more year. Please, Lord? Please..."

I felt I was begging more than believing.

Moose was too weak to get into the truck on his own power, so we bundled him up in his favorite blanket and placed him in the vehicle. At last we began the terrible trek to the vet's office. But the moment we got there, Moose began to wake up. He was suddenly alert and energetic. Moose climbed out of the truck on his own power, and he started acting like he wanted to play. He walked normally, wagging his tail, straining on his leash, and covering us with kisses.

I knew that when dogs go to the pound or vet clinic, they often get excited by the scents of other animals. They enter a world of sensory stimuli, and they pay attention to everything, so I felt no reason to be overly optimistic about his behavior.

By the time we actually walked into the vet's office, however, he was acting like his big, goofy, Moosey self. The vet's assistant tried to put him on the scale (the drug that was going to be used to put him to sleep is adjusted for body weight), but he jumped off and ran toward me, as if saying, "I don't like standing on scales any more than you do."

After the vet left the room to prepare the injection, Rob and I began to question ourselves.

"I don't know about this. I mean, look at him," I said. "He's acting kinda normal."

"Moose, come," Rob said. Moose trotted over happily. They looked into each other's eyes for a moment. Then Rob turned to me. "Maybe we need a second opinion."

When we brought this up with the vet, he said, "The type of tumor removed from him is not one that would metastasize. But given his age and health problems, putting him to sleep might still be best."

"Okay," Rob said, "but is that what you would do if this was your dog and he was acting like this right now?"

The vet studied Moose for a moment and surprised us by suggesting we tentatively postpone putting him to sleep. He gave him an antibiotic and prescribed some follow-up medicines, but he didn't want to give us false hope. "You can try this, but you might be back in a couple of days."

Rob and I were stunned as we drove back home with Moose—a cautious celebration. And then a lightbulb went off in my head. (But only a 60-watt. A 150-watt would require more brain capacity than I had.) My mind was drawn back to the phone call, only two days earlier, when Sharon told me about a miraculous healing. "The battle isn't over yet," she had said. *Was that a word from God for us about Moose? God was talking about a dog? Surely, healing people is far more important—why would He care?*

When we got him home, Moose started gobbling up his food, and the next day I watched him romp around with Willow in our backyard. Sharon's words gave me peace, and I was convinced that he had, indeed, been healed. Moose was going to be fine for at least a year. *Man! I should've asked for three!*

I called Sharon immediately and told her about our Miracle Moose. "You're not crazy!" I said.

"I know," she replied with a chuckle.

* * * * * * * *

I don't know why we are always so surprised when God does what He says He will do—like heal, speak to prophets, give spiritual gifts, or give words of knowledge. But it's silly to limit God.

Sometimes we become the casting director and look at the picture of the circumstances in front of us and say, "Nope. This is impossible for God to do anything with." So we don't even extend an opportunity in prayer for God to come in and show us what He can do. We don't invite Him into our situations.

Based on Moose's appearance, he was as good as gone. But we still prayed and asked God to show up and intervene. Even though I felt like I was begging and not believing, I asked Him to come into the situation and change the story—because that's what He asks us to do. He wants us to bring Him into *everything*. Whether it's a sick relative or a final exam, He wants us to involve Him, and once we do—well, after that it's all up to Him.

He also wants us to persist in our prayers—not to give up on God's power to transform. When I was a teenager, the teacher who told me he expected nothing from me was wrong. He tried to censor my entire life based on my performance in his class. But Ms. Lackman believed in my possibilities. She gave me a chance, and my mother was the same way. She never gave up, even as she bailed her 16-year-old stoner son out of jail for a DUI.

From all appearances at that time in my life, I should have been written off. Thankfully, my mom was a God-seeking woman of prayer. "I don't know what's wrong with my son, but God, I know You can change him and make him into the man he needs to be, so I'm just going to keep praying, and I'm not giving up!"

And I'm sure she closed her prayer in her best Clint Eastwood voice, informing God, "I'll be watching for You."

I believe it was my mother's persistent prayers that changed things. I could be in a prison cell right now instead of writing this book. That's why I feel qualified to say that if you feel called by God to do something but your circumstances and obstacles make it look impossible, *so what?* We have a big God, and He can fulfill that calling.

If you're hurting, God has something for you. In Matthew 11:28, Jesus gives a command and then a promise: "Come to me, all you who are weary and burdened, and I will give you rest."

Inviting Jesus in and knowing that He's in charge is ultimately what allows us to rest. And frankly, some of us could really use the beauty sleep.

MIRACLE MOOSE. This photo was taken a few months after Moose's miraculous recovery.

14

HOLD THE MAYO

Hearing a voice from above is something we all hope for. But hearing a voice from below? Not so much. The good news was that this voice from below was coming from Rob. The bad news was that he seemed upset about something.

Rob is a talented carpenter, and for two weeks he had been busy building a new island for the kitchen. I was just starting to empty the dishwasher when I heard him open the garage door from downstairs and yell up to me in a panic.

"Torry! I need mayonnaise! Quick!"

Not certain I was hearing correctly, I confirmed what I heard him say. "Mayonnaise?" I yelled questioningly back down to him from the kitchen.

"YES!" Rob bellowed rather emphatically. "Mayonnaise! QUICK!" He slammed the garage door shut with a bang.

I rifled through the cupboards for the mayo while mentally running through a myriad of reasons why he would need it so badly. *What constitutes a mayonnaise emergency in a garage?*

Then I hesitated in my Search for the Great White Mayo. Rob hadn't specified which type of mayonnaise he wanted, and it could make all the difference in the world. *Does he want the extra-large container of mayo from Sam's Club that's in the fridge? Or the new mayo with olive oil that I purchased last week? Or maybe he wants the low-fat mayonnaise I keep pushed far to the back of the fridge because it tastes like a mix between glue and cornstarch. Wait! Maybe he wants his own personal squeezable container of Miracle Whip that he reserves only for his hot dogs. But Miracle Whip is technically classified as salad dressing...*

(*Door opens.*) "Hurry up! I need mayonnaise! NOW!"

SLAM!

Quickly, I grabbed all the assorted mayonnaise jars to avoid making two trips in case I got the wrong one. (I hate stairs.)

My arms were loaded as I carefully negotiated the steps without the use of the handrails. Using my chin to hold the small, squeezable Miracle Whip on top of the large mayo underneath required some careful balance. Upon reaching the garage door, I had to fumble to turn the doorknob. I was certain that Rob could hear me trying to get the door open, and I was irritated that he hadn't opened it for me from the other side. Finally, I managed to open the door and catch it with my elbow so I could somewhat stumble in.

"You could've helped with the door, ya know!" I said in a condescending tone. I couldn't actually see him because my chin was pointing toward the floor to hold the squeeze bottle.

When I looked up, I saw that Rob appeared rather pale and stared at me with an expression I didn't recognize. He lifted his hand to show me his reason for not helping with the door. "I can't. I'm bleeding."

"Oh," I replied, slowly processing the large amount of blood I was seeing drip from his finger. "Why'd you want the mayonnaise?"

Staring at the four various-sized jars of mayo nestled in my arms, he S-L-O-W-L-Y said, "Band-Aids."

Feeling like an idiot, I scurried off for the Band-Aids, with questions popping in my head like firecrackers. *Does he want the Batman Band-Aids from my bathroom? Or the regular Band-Aids from the kitchen? Or the larger size Band-Aids from the closet?*

I think this story is funny, and to be honest, there's no real moral to it, other than sometimes we get stuff wrong. And injured people should learn to enunciate. And when it comes to mayonnaise, you should have plenty of options.

FIREPROOF. There is really no reason for this picture to be in the book, but I had an empty spot to fill, and I'd like to show that I'm not the only one who does stupid things. This is what happens when you pour the last of the gas from a five-gallon can directly into a burn barrel. Rob thought the coals in the barrel were out, but when the gas hit the embers, it ignited and followed the fumes to the can, causing it to explode in his face. Thankfully, he was all right, but boy, was his face red! And so were his hands...and shoulders...and ears...and....

15
HISSING FITS

My fear of snakes originated in the bathtub. You may have seen this on an episode of *World's Most Traumatizing Pranks*. It aired last Thursday on the Terrible Parenting Channel.

I was six years old, happily soaking with Mr. Bubble and my rubber ducky, when my dad and brother interrupted my personal spa time by hurling a garter snake into the tub. They cackled when I leaped out and sprinted into the living room, leaving a trail of bubbles in my wake. Right behind me chased my brother, holding the soap-covered snake by the tail.

"It's just a garter snake!" he yelled. "It's not going to hurt you."

I didn't hear the last part until I was already standing out in the yard, buck naked and dripping Mr. Bubble.

Decades later, this scene would pass through my mind on a trip to South Africa, where I was filming a movie. Imagine my terror when I overheard two film-crew members talking.

"They caught a boomslang last night," Crew Member One said.

"Really? A tree snake? Where?" said Crew Member Two.

"Balcony of room B."

I looked down at my lodge room key. "B."

"Who's staying in 'B'?" Crew Member Two asked.

"The big guy with the red hair."

"Should we tell him?"

"No. He's American. Besides, I think I saw him on last night's episode of *World's Most Traumatizing Pranks*. We may find him in the fetal position in his closet."

After I uncurled myself and emerged from my closet, I was on high alert for snakes everywhere I went. If something brushed my hair, I would leap nearly five inches out of my chair (which was four and a half inches higher than my best vertical jump in high school).

South Africa has all sorts of poisonous serpents—the puff adder, Cape cobra, spitting cobra, and of course the dreaded black mamba. If the fangs of a black mamba strike a vein or main artery, a person can be dead in 20 minutes. God definitely knew what He was doing when He designed the black mamba's head in the shape of a coffin.

I know the word "boomslang" sounds like a cross between a drumline and a rap group, but don't be deceived. They're extremely deadly. In fact, the only thing more horrifying than a boomslang on my balcony was the sorry state of the screenplay for the movie I was about to act in.

After arriving in Africa, I was shocked to discover that the screenplay wasn't even close to being finished. Fearing that the director would want us to improvise many of the scenes, I volunteered to help rewrite it. For free. Of all the dumb things I've done in my life, that was one of the dumbest.

While I was in Africa, I was in the middle of writing this book, so I was already thinking about the theme of our calling, which is what the Bible story of Esther is all about. So I found myself trying to turn the screenplay into a modern-day retelling of Esther. Imagine my surprise when the director informed me that he needed the python scene ASAP.

"What python scene? Esther never wrestled with a python."

"The snake wrangler is coming tomorrow, and we need that scene."

"Again—*why* do we need a python?"

"It's already been paid for," he replied calmly, as if it made perfect sense.

I studied him for a moment before responding. "Didja keep the receipt? Maybe you can get a refund and put it toward the screenplay."

I went ahead and wrote a riveting scene where a python lurks in an African jungle while I am safely doing laundry in my house in Tennessee. But the director wasn't buying it. He wanted me in the scene with the python. I was worried I would end up *in* the python.

Not having much choice, I wrote a scene in which four characters are having a picnic and sitting on the ground in a circle, and one of them is completely oblivious to the fact that a 12-foot python is sliding along the ground within striking range.

Of the four characters in this scene, two were supposed to be rangers, so that left either me or my friend and talented costar, Melody, to play the character who was afraid of snakes.

"I'm not acting with a python!" Melody exclaimed.

"Why not?" I asked.

"The first woman to share top billing with a snake was Eve, and look how that turned out!"

"Exactly. It's your chance to right a wrong. I personally believe it's your duty as a woman to do so."

"Not happening!"

"Why not? It's a man-eating python, not a woman-eating python."

My argument was unconvincing, so the role fell to me, and the next day I found myself heading to the set to do the dreaded python scene. I just needed to make a small detour to the wardrobe department first to see if they carried Depends.

During the entire scene, I had to pretend to be focused on the food while enjoying the picnic. We were all in a hurry for the scene to be over, but it had to be reshot again and again and again. This python was a bit of a diva and wouldn't cooperate. I was seated on a log while the snake wrangler placed the python behind me. At one point, the restless snake had to be gently scolded. No one wants a freshly punished python lurking behind them. The wrangler was aware of my fear, and he tried to keep me calm by saying, "Don't look. Don't turn around, Torry. Oh…ah…ah…uh-oh…DO NOT LOOK BACK."

Allow me to take a moment here to talk about the wonderful product that Depends is.

The scene was supposed to go like this. We're sitting in a circle when a python sneaks up behind me. Everyone sees it but me. Without making any sudden moves or noises, they motion to me what's happening, but I'm too busy running my mouth to see their gestures or hear their warnings. Finally, I turn toward the snake and see that it's only a few feet from my face. Melody and I are then supposed to dash for the Jeep, where she jumps in ahead of me and I pile in after her.

The director yelled, "Action," and I began my lines. When it came time for me to turn toward the snake, it was WAY closer than just a few feet. I could feel the snake's breath on my face and hear its hiss.

I froze for a moment as the snake sized me up. He probably thought, *Could I swallow him whole? If I did, I'd be a hero back at python school. And I may never have to eat again in my life!*

At the end of the scene, Melody and I sprint for the vehicle, but I left that woman in the dust. As I approached the safari Jeep, I leaped onto the running board to propel myself into the vehicle, but I didn't quite get there. I made it only halfway into the passenger seat, while the other half of me dangled outside, my feet flailing and pedaling in the air like a cartoon character. Melody had to shove and shove and SHOVE my derriere to get me into the Jeep, like trying to stuff a water buffalo into a clown car. When I finally sat upright in the Jeep, I looked back to see the entire crew chuckling, including the python. I slithered back to my lair to write, praying that the director hadn't ordered a lion-wrestling scene for the next day.

I guess I didn't pray hard enough.

The next day I watched a 400-pound male lion spring onto the man right in front of me. I watched in awe as they tumbled to the ground in a mass of claws and fur. I was less than 50 yards away, but

I was still close enough for the lion to order me as a side dish if one man wasn't enough to satisfy his appetite. Yanking out my iPhone, I turned to the nearest expert on lion diets. "Siri, how many men can a lion eat in one sitting?"

"Did you know that the lion is one of the fiercest creatures on earth?" said Siri. "This hungry hunter needs at least 11 pounds of meat each day and can devour as much as 70 pounds in one sitting."

That's 280 Quarter Pounders! (My OCD compelled me to do the calculations. Actually, my OCD compelled Rob to do the calculations. I hate math. For me, the most important qualities in a friend are character and math ability, and Rob has all three.)

Thankfully, this particular lion wasn't really feasting. It was frolicking.

One of the scenes in the movie called for a lion to attack a ranger. The sound of growls and roars would be added later, giving the viewer the illusion that the big cat was trying to use this ranger to meet his daily requirement for protein. In truth, the lion was just having a good time playing with his buddy, a well-known lion handler.

This lion handler tumbles around with lions like they're house cats. In fact, he trusts lions so much that sometimes he sleeps with them. The old bedtime prayer must hold special meaning for him: "Now I lay me down to sleep, I pray the Lord my soul to keep. If I should die before I wake...Never mind."

I don't think I could ever put aside my fears and place my trust in a lion, especially not after talking to the lion handler's assistant. During the filming of the attack scene, I sidled up to the assistant and asked him if he'd ever wrestled with lions himself.

"Once," he told me, pulling down his collar to reveal an ugly five-inch scar at the top of his neck.

He explained that he had pestered the lion handler with the persistence of a tsetse fly until he was finally given the chance to work with the big cat. He wasn't as confident as his boss, however, and the lion sensed his fear and raked his claws across his neck, nearly costing him his life.

Hearing this story makes it even harder for me to wrap my mind around the famous passage in Isaiah 11:6 that talks about the wolf lying down with the lamb. (And yes, even though you've probably heard it was a lion lying down with the lamb, it was really a wolf.) Wolf...lion...as Rob would say, "Whatever." The point is that in God's future kingdom, peace will reign, even between lions and lambs and between snakes and me. Predictably, some people with a secular mindset don't buy it. One famous filmmaker quipped, "The lion will lay down with the lamb, but the lamb won't get much sleep."

But still, I believe it'll happen.

Most people probably assume that for the lion to lie down with the lamb, the lion must become meek and mild. But as the great writer G.K. Chesterton once pointed out, that is grossly unfair to the lion.

"The real problem is—Can the lion lie down with the lamb and still retain his royal ferocity?" Chesterton asks in his book *Orthodoxy*.

The answer is yes. And that's the miracle of it all.

Just as we assume the lion becomes meek when it hangs out with the lamb, many of us ignore the complete character of God. We focus only on His loving side at the cost of ignoring His righteousness. Everyone likes the image of gentle Jesus, but they forget that He also rebukes demons, turns over the tables of the money changers in the temple, and gets furious with the Pharisees, comparing them to a brood of vipers. (Snakes again!)

The lion and the lamb represent both sides of Christ. He is the sacrificial lamb, but He is also the Lion of Judah, and He protects us against Satan, who lurks behind us like a 12-foot python slithering along the South African soil.

Trust is the key to a lion handler's relationship with these majestic creatures, and trust is the key to our calling from the Lord. Do we trust God enough to do whatever He asks of us and to go wherever

He sends us, even if it means entering a lion's den and sleeping with one of those ferocious animals?

Hmm. Maybe. But I wouldn't fight him for the blanket.

Snakes on the Plain. The only thing more frightening than the flip-flop shirt I'm wearing is that 12-foot python behind me. The snake wrangler is demonstrating how to work with the python and has just said, "She's acting moody today"—not the most encouraging words to hear when setting up for another take.

16
SPECIAL DELIVERY

I made my way down the long, pitch-dark trail leading from the lodge to the film set in Africa when I suddenly heard a cacophony of baboon shrieks coming from the jungle around me.

They had perfected their bloodcurdling screams, making Ozzy Osbourne sound like a country crooner. I'm not really fluent in baboon, but I had a feeling their screams could be translated, "Kill the redhead! The fat will add flavor!"

Being defenseless against a band of baboons, I brought along a banana to use as a bribe. *This should keep them from tearing my face off.* But after walking 500 feet, I figured I deserved a reward. Next thing you know, there was only a peel. Worst-case scenario, I could hurl the peel at them, and they'd slip on it, giving me time to run. The banana was actually a plantain, which is much larger and very bland and mushy. Personally, I thought I was doing the baboons a favor by eating it.

Working in a third world country with a third-rate screenplay on three hours of sleep per night has a way of stressing a person out. The combination of being sleep deprived, overworked, and in constant fear of attacking baboons kept my anxiety at an all-time high. On this particular morning, I had a splitting headache and took five aspirins to shake it. I know, I know... that sounds like a lot, but I don't like pain. Or, as it turns out, baboons.

To make matters worse, I had opted to skip breakfast so I could keep writing the scene we'd be doing later in the day. To fight my hunger pains, I had dipped into a half-filled bag of Thai spice potato chips left over from the night before. It wasn't the perfect morning meal, but it was a nice break from what we normally had—a plate of mush that the South Africans called "pap," or sometimes "slap pap," probably because you want to slap your pap every time you take a bite. Devouring the Thai spice chips on an empty stomach gave me a severe case of heartburn, so I took five antacids.

Don't look at me like that. I told you, I don't like pain.

And then there were the malaria pills. I took only one of those. Before leaving America, the nurse had warned me that *some* people experience hallucinations when taking the malaria pills, but I dismissed her.

"Skinny people, sure. I doubt it'll have an effect like that on a guy my size," I said. Heavy people are more grounded. Literally. They sink into the ground more.

Needless to say, I was one miserable, frazzled man as I staggered along the dark trail guided only by my meager flashlight. I was relieved when I reached the movie set and finally found light—and lots of it. We were filming a bonfire scene, so the place was ablaze.

The director's plan was to film all kinds of little scenes of various people around the bonfire, which was enclosed by what South Africans call a "boma." That's when my body finally decided enough was enough, and I became extremely cold. Even though I was huddled close to the bonfire, my body began shivering uncontrollably.

"Are you okay?" Melody asked. I was shaking so hard I looked like a bowl of red Jell-O in an earthquake. I couldn't even say my lines without shivering, so some of the crew members piled blankets on me between takes.

"We've gotta get you back to your room," one person said.

"Something's wrong," added another.

I brushed away the concern. "I'm f-f-f-f-fine. Just film the s-s-s-s-scene!"

I didn't want to be responsible for fouling up the film's shooting schedule, so I was determined to ignore my misery. Plus, the sooner we finished this movie, the sooner I could get out of South Africa. But when my vision began to blur, the director became concerned. He insisted that some crew members rush me back to the lodge and into my bed.

All I wanted was for them to leave me alone with my anguish, but they were justifiably worried and not about to desert me. Three of the six crew members were prayer warriors on the movie set, but while they were busy praying for me, I was busy praying they'd just leave me alone.

"I'm telling you I'm f-f-f-f-fine! Just leave me alone with the ceiling fan," I said, looking up. "He seems friendly. Look! He's waving."

Then things really got weird. People's faces started shape-shifting, coming closer, pulling back, and then looming closer again. It was like I was looking at everyone through a transparent lava lamp.

Suddenly I went from being cold and shivering to being *hot* and shivering. And I mean really, really hot. I felt like I was on fire. "I gotta get out of these clothes! Now!"

Of course, with four women in the room, that wasn't going to happen. They may have been praying with their eyes closed, but there's always a peeker.

My prayer warriors were not about to budge, especially when it looked like I was having a mental meltdown. They doubled down on their prayers instead, getting even louder, while others tried to calm me.

Andy, the executive producer who also owned the game preserve where we were filming, was seated beside my bed. "Shhh, shhh. It's all okay. You're going to be fine," he said in a whisper meant to reassure and calm me.

"Could you pleeease get the girls out of here? I've gotta get these clothes off!"

Suddenly their praying got even louder and more desperate— probably because they feared they were going to see me with my clothes off.

That's when Andy's assistant had an idea. "Hey! How about you unbuckle your jeans and unzip them? Then just lift your hips up, and I'll grab your pant legs and yank them off under the blankets."

"But there's girls!" I objected.

"You can stay under the blanket. No one will see."

I wanted to argue, but his face had just shape-shifted into that of a baboon. *There's a baboon by my bed!* I was freaking out, but I knew I needed to stay calm. If he sensed fear, he'd attack.

"Just unbuckle your belt," the baboon said. "Trust me."

I needed to show the baboon that I was cooperative, so I whispered, "I trust you."

While I was fiddling with my pants buckle beneath the blankets, Andy continued to assure me I was going to be okay. He was probably thinking I had *better* be okay because our nearest medical facility was a first-aid kit. If this became a full-blown emergency, they would have to call in a helicopter from 40 minutes away.

I kept my eyes on the baboon while Andy attempted to calm me by saying one of the most random things I've ever heard—and I have ADHD, so I'm an expert in random.

"Don't worry. You'll be fine," he said.

"Are you a doctor?" I asked.

"No, but I've delivered babies before."

What? He delivers babies? What's that got to do with anything? Why is he babbling about birthing babies...unless—oh my word—is THAT what's happening?

Since the baboon at the foot of my bed could apparently speak English, I wondered if maybe it could teach me Lamaze. (The only breathing exercises I had ever done were when I took the stairs.) I quickly unbuckled and unzipped my pants and declared, "Okay, I'm ready!"

I'm not sure why I wasn't more alarmed that a baboon was yanking on my pant legs, but it pulled my jeans straight out from under the blanket in one smooth move. The next thing I knew, it was holding up my pants upside down.

I stared at the trousers in horror.

"Cut the umbilical cord!" I shouted, convinced that I had just given birth to a pair of jeans. "It's wrapped around his head!"

"That's your belt."

I will name him Levi.

"I think you're having an anxiety attack," Andy said reassuringly, which did nothing to reassure me.

An anxiety attack? I've never had one of those before. Am I going to start having them all the time now? And more importantly, am I going to give birth to pants every time I feel anxious? I can't afford to raise that much denim!

It took a good couple of hours for me to come back to earth and begin to feel like myself again.

I also learned that Andy really did know how to deliver babies. Most of the people who run game preserves and farms out in the bush have to be medically trained in a lot of areas because the nearest hospital is so far away.

The next day, I was feeling good enough to get back to working on the screenplay with a fellow writer. He told me how scary the incident had been.

"Do you have any idea what might have caused it?" he asked.

"No idea at all. Unless it was the malaria pills."

Then my fellow writer picked up my malaria pill bottle and said, "Did you have anything else with them? What did you have for breakfast?"

"Just some Thai chips. Oh, and five antacids and five aspirin."

He looked at the bottom of the prescription label. "Warning: Do not take with aspirin or antacids."

Huh. Well, that explains everything. If I'd taken the time to read the directions in the first place, none of this ever would've happened. But as a person with ADHD, reading warning labels isn't really my thing. I blame it on the pharmaceutical companies. If they want somebody like me to read their labels, they should put a joke at the end as a reward for reading all the boring stuff.

• • • • • • • • •

I learned the hard way that failing to heed warnings can be risky medically. It can also be risky spiritually. I believe that God speaks to us in many ways, but the primary way is through the Bible. Scripture is loaded with warnings from God, and if you ignore them, you do so at your own peril—like when the prophet Jeremiah kept warning the Israelites to turn back to God. But they were quick to ignore him, so they were quick to be conquered and were dragged off to distant lands—exactly as Jeremiah had warned.

We often read the Bible the same way I read medicine labels. We skip the boring parts (my apologies to Leviticus). But with selective reading, we miss some of the most important passages, including God's warnings to us.

If you're serious about following your call, you'll be serious about following God's Word first—*all of it*. So for heaven's sake, heed the warnings and don't be a baboon.

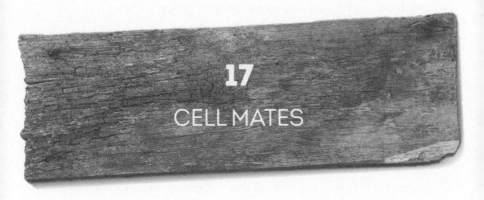

17

CELL MATES

frica was beautiful. The sunsets were glorious, the trees so unique and picturesque. At least that's how it looked on the postcard I sent home—I hardly got to see any of that in person. I was stuck in my room, writing the script. I felt like a prisoner chained to my computer.

In a lot of ways, prison might have been better. At least there you could recognize the meat you were being served. Countless times I inquired about the fatty gray substance on my plate.

"It's gazelle."

"It's boar."

"It's kudu."

I had no idea if kudu was animal, vegetable, mineral, gas, liquid, or solid, much less whether it was even food.

You're also allowed to make a phone call from jail. Where we were in South Africa, there was no cell service. I could only hold my phone up and look at it longingly, wishing I could go to the Apple store and get an upgrade to two cans and string.

In prison, I should add, you get yard exercise with a 75 percent chance of coming back alive. With all of the crime and carnivores in

South Africa, your survival rate drops to 35 percent. I felt sorry for the prison-striped zebras. They were obviously lifers.

I was trapped in a compound behind security gates, and even if I had tried to make an escape, I had no vehicle. I made special note of where the keys to the Jeep were kept, just in case I needed to make my escape. *I can crash through the gates to get to the airport if things get any worse. But I'll have to floor it the whole way, or I'll get carjacked.*

I was thankful when I learned that the cast had been invited on a private safari on our one day off, but I was hesitant to go. I felt like I needed to keep writing. But as I watched the others climbing into the Jeep, I realized this might be my only opportunity to bust out.

"Shotgun!" I shouted, diving for the front seat.

* * * * * * * * *

The narrow, dusty road wound its way through the wide expanse of waist-high grassland as we headed out to see the elephants. We drove through hundreds of acres on the Welgevonden Game Reserve with wildlife everywhere—a veritable Eden on all sides. We saw hippos, lions, giraffes, cheetahs, leopards, and more. I was thrilled to be riding in the front seat of the green safari Jeep, right next to the ranger.

The ranger parked the Jeep about 50 yards away from a herd of elephants, but I wanted close-up photographs.

"Can't we move a little closer?" I asked.

"No, they might charge," the ranger said.

"Hmm…maybe we should back up."

The ranger said we were fine where we were, and he was right. These elephants weren't charging. In fact, they weren't doing anything at all. I was hoping for some action shots.

"These guys are boring. Where are the artistic ones?" I asked.

The ranger squinted at me. "Artistic?"

"Elephants love to paint! Don't you know that?" I said, pleased with myself. He had been educating me the entire trip, and now it was finally my turn to show off my expert knowledge of zoology.

"Where've you seen an elephant paint?" he asked.

"Alaska. I think the cold releases their creativity. Or maybe they're just bored. Winters in Alaska are kinda dull. I know one guy who made a life-size nativity scene out of toothpicks. He even made a donkey and a couple of camels."

"Can we get back to the painting elephant?" the ranger asked.

"Sure," I said. "Feel free to take notes."

I proceeded to tell him all about Annabelle the elephant, a lovable creature I had met while living in Alaska. Annabelle was the star of the zoo in Anchorage. She was the Picasso of pachyderms, and she had created more than 600 works of art, which sold for hundreds of dollars each.

It was 1993, and I was a host for the Fox Kids Club on Anchorage television when I first interacted with Annabelle. I stood by her, dressed in my brand-spanking-new white bib overalls, taping a spot about her artistic ability. As I began to tape my intro, Annabelle was getting ready to paint a picture on the blank canvas. She gripped an oversized paintbrush in her trunk and eyed the five-gallon buckets of paint in front of her—green, blue, red, and yellow.

"Welcome to the Fox 4 Kids Club," I said as the camera began to roll. "Today, we're at the Alaska Zoo visiting our friend Annabelle the elephant!"

In my peripheral vision, I spotted a long gray trunk swinging directly toward me, wielding a paintbrush. Before I could dodge it, Annabelle swiped a long streak of green paint straight across my chest. The paintbrush hit me so hard that I stumbled. Annabelle had mistaken my white overalls for the biggest canvas she'd ever seen, and the temptation was too much for her to resist.

"Annabelle, no!" the trainer scolded.

But even with her enormous ears, Annabelle had selective hearing. This mischievous elephant was not done with her spontaneous bit of performance art, so she dipped the brush in the bucket of red paint and slapped me again, this time on the side.

The trainer tried to correct her, but by now my new overalls were already ruined, so why not let her keep going? *This will make great TV!* Besides, Annabelle's works of art sold for hundreds of dollars, and I figured my overalls had suddenly shot up in value.

Annabelle was a prize elephant, and not just because she painted. She was an actual prize. Crown Zellerbach, a local paper company, sponsored a promotional contest in 1968 to see who could sell the most tissues. A grocery store owner from Anchorage, Jack Snyder, won the contest, and he was given a choice between receiving either $3,000 or his own baby elephant.

For Snyder, it was an easy decision. Seriously. Who wouldn't want a baby elephant?

Initially, Snyder kept Annabelle in the grocery store parking lot—not your everyday sight when picking up food for the week. But with the severe Alaska winter coming fast, he made arrangements for Annabelle to live in a heated stall on the ranch of a lady named Sammye Seawell.

In an article in *Senior Voice*, Seawell recalled how she would draw stunned expressions from passersby as she took Annabelle out on walks along O'Malley Road. People were probably even more stunned when they saw the size of the waste bag she pulled out of her pocket. The elephant even bonded with Sammye's Newfoundland dog, Woofie. Annabelle would stand on Woofie's tail so the poor dog couldn't leave her side. (She probably would've been even more useful than an ATM at keeping our dog Moose in the yard.)

"There were so many people coming to see an elephant—an elephant in Alaska—and there wasn't a place big enough for the crowds," Seawell said in *Senior Voice*. "So the idea for the zoo evolved."

Seawell started the Alaska Zoo in Anchorage, and Annabelle was among the first group of animals when it opened in 1969. You can still find photos of Annabelle as a young elephant at the zoo wearing mukluk boots on each of her feet—a must for any elephant in Alaska but a definite fashion faux pas for elephants in Africa. The foot sweat would be unbearable.

After I told the safari guide about Annabelle, he gently pointed out that African elephants didn't exactly have a thriving arts community in the wild.

"Probably because the paint stores are too far away," I supposed.

"Or because wild elephants *don't paint*."

"Oh, yeah? Then how do you explain the one holding the paintbrush?"

"That's a tree."

I took my glasses out of my pocket and put them on. He was right. The elephant had just uprooted a tree and flung it at another. Finally, some action! I was awed by the overwhelming power of these animals. *This is what Annabelle should've been doing—being an elephant, not painting.*

· · · · · · · · ·

I couldn't help but wonder what it must have been like for Annabelle, born in India, to be taken to a strange land like Alaska. Elephants have huge brains and long memories, so she must've remembered her time in her homeland. Being in captivity so far from home was probably the elephant equivalent of being Joseph in the Old Testament.

Joseph had been taken into captivity after his jealous brothers sold him to a caravan of hairy Ishmaelites who carried him to Egypt. However, as anyone familiar with the Genesis story knows, Joseph flourished in Egypt. He had a knack for interpreting dreams, and when he warned Pharaoh about an impending famine, the ruler released him from prison and put him in charge as his second in command.

Being in prison certainly wasn't in Joseph's original plans, and it's quite possible that many of us feel like our lives aren't meeting expectations either. Just like me in Africa, maybe you feel trapped in your job or mired in the demands of everyday life.

I was cooped up in a metaphorical prison, writing away on the script. I desperately wanted to make a break for it and run into the open arms of Jesus, but I didn't think I could squeeze through my prison bars to get to Him. Besides, I felt like God was my heavenly prison warden and was refusing me parole. I know that sounds harsh, but even Jesus had a moment when He felt abandoned. "My God, my God, why have you forsaken me?" (Matthew 27:46).

That's exactly how I felt. But in hindsight, I see it now. God was keeping me there because that's where He wanted me to be. I didn't like the discomfort, the snakes, the baboons, or the food, and if I had a tin cup, I would've been banging it on my bars. But if Joseph's story tells us anything, it's that God's plans for our lives are always better than our own, no matter how dire things look.

When life got difficult for me as a young man, I fled to Alaska as my way of escaping. But to my surprise, I ran right into Jesus, who captured my heart, and my life was never the same again. Kinda weird how that worked out. Or, more likely, it was kind of God to work it out for me. All of that to say, if Annabelle can learn to paint in captivity in the cold land of Alaska, if Joseph can rise up from an Egyptian prison, and if I can choke down a mouthful of kudu in Africa without throwing up, then you too can flourish anywhere God places you.

Wherever we are, God is calling, but beware. When you least expect it, He might just smack you across the chest like a 9,000-pound elephant wielding a paintbrush. Not to worry, however. God knows something about works of art. In fact, as far as He's concerned, you're His Rembrandt, while I'm more His finger painting—and we're all a part of the masterpiece that He's been painting since the beginning of time.

PAINTING WITH PACHYDERMS. This is moments before Annabelle gave me the great brush-off. Of all the elephants I've worked with, she's my favorite.

MONKEY BUSINESS. I wanted to get a picture with a baboon, but it wasn't worth putting my life at risk. So this is Suesa, a chimp whose original guardian was Michael Jackson. When I was younger, I met Suesa at my parents' Easter egg hunt, and we just happened to be wearing identical clothing—red and yellow shirts with *Miami Vice* straight-up collars. Obviously, Suesa had excellent fashion sense—just like Michael and me.

18

FALLING SHORT

This ice-breaker question always comes up at parties: What's your most embarrassing moment? I now have an answer. And in case I'm ever asked, I also have an answer to another question: What's your most embarrassing moment in front of 50,000 people?

I'm on the International Christian Visual Media (ICVM) board, and I was attending the annual conference in Covington, Kentucky, when my momentous moment occurred. One of the reasons I was voted onto the board is that I'm addicted to networking. I had come up with the idea of a Networking Night Walk, where we could talk and exchange business cards as we strolled from Covington to Cincinnati across the beautiful John A. Roebling Suspension Bridge.

If you happened to meet a great new contact, you could stop along the way and talk. If you got tired of a conversation, you could just walk faster than the other person. And if a conversation really went poorly, you could jump off the bridge entirely. I made a mental note to grab the life preserver from my trunk, just in case.

We had just completed a field trip that included lunch at the Creation Museum, and by the time I returned to the hotel, I was running behind. That's when my cell phone rang.

"Where are you?" asked Diane, the ICVM president. "Everybody's waiting for you in the lobby."

"I'm almost there. I just want to run to my room and change clothes first," I said.

"There's no time for that. People are getting restless. We need you here now."

I had hoped to switch out of my cargo shorts, which chafed my legs—more information than you probably want to know. (It was my right leg specifically, three and one-quarter inches up from the knee.) I also wanted to empty my pockets, which were jammed with my cell phone, a fat wallet, and my massive key ring, which could've served as a ship's anchor. I also had a special edition Swiss Army knife with extra features, including can opener, pliers, screwdriver, nail file—basically, everything but a pop-up camper. In short, my pockets were packed for the apocalypse in case I couldn't get anywhere near my car trunk. (Seriously, people, when that thing comes, you gotta be prepared. You never know when you're going to need to get a manicure, pull a tooth, or whittle a full-size canoe.)

Setting comfort and chafing aside, I changed my plan of action and headed straight for the lobby. When I got there, I found that the ICVM president was right. The lobby was packed, and people were getting impatient.

About 50 people had decided to do the walk, the summer evening was glorious, and most importantly, I got to spend time with my good friend and *New York Times* bestselling author Tosca Lee. (Did you notice how casually I dropped her name and credits? Yeah, I'm pretty much known for my tact and subtlety.)

Anyway, I was pretty impressed with myself. After all, Tosca Lee was not only the author of books such as *Iscariot* and *Havah* but also the first runner-up in the Mrs. United States pageant in 1998.

I was starstruck. I was already a fanboy of Tosca before I met her, and the idea of someone like me being friends with someone like her would have been unbelievable to young Torry. But now, so many years later, my world had changed, and being friends with Tosca Lee was like the class nerd becoming friends with the prom queen. I was having a great time as we strolled by Smale Riverfront Park, adjacent to the suspension bridge. I sang in my head, *Look at me, I'm Torry De. Walking next to Tosca Lee! What gorgeous hair, such a good-looking pair…I'll bet they use Pantene!*

As we were walking, Tosca suddenly noticed a 20-foot-long keyboard spread out on the park grounds. If you've seen the Tom Hanks movie *Big*, you probably remember him jumping onto a humongous keyboard, leaping from key to key as he played "Chopsticks." That is exactly the kind of piano Tosca spotted in the park.

"Let's play the piano!" she exclaimed.

If you knew anything about Tosca (but you probably don't because you're not her friend and *I am*), you'd know she is a classically trained pianist and ballerina. We have so much in common. If I could've found someone strong enough to catch me when I leaped, I could've been a ballerina too.

"You go ahead," I said. "I'll just admire your fancy footwork from afar."

"No way, wallflower," she said. "You're playing it with me. All you have to do is step on one note when I tell you."

"One note?"

"Yup, just one."

"That sounds easy."

"Yes, but you'll have to play it twice."

"Okay, now it's getting complicated."

"I'll walk you through it," she said with a smile.

And so it began. Tosca started to play the *Star Wars* theme song, stepping onto the first key with her left foot and hopping to the right for the next key. But that key didn't make a sound because she wasn't heavy enough.

"Jump on it harder!" I said. Suddenly, I was an expert on the foot piano. (Sometimes my confidence exceeds my abilities.) As she continued to hop and play and hop some more, she pointed at me, and I stepped forward with my right foot.

DING!

I played the note perfectly. George Lucas would have been impressed.

By this time, a small crowd had gathered to watch our virtuoso performance. Tosca continued to step and play, step and play, and then she pointed at me—my cue once again to amaze the world with my footwork. I eagerly stepped forward, and then...

Time froze.

Or maybe the freezing sensation was actually the cool breeze that I suddenly felt against my legs. To my horror, my cargo shorts had fallen to my ankles—something I'm pretty sure never happened to Beethoven.

Fortunately, my long, untucked shirt provided me with the cover I needed as I very quickly scooted backward and then turned and ran, all while trying desperately to raise my shorts.

With the combined weight of my wallet, car keys, cell phone, massive key ring, special edition Swiss Army knife with extra features (including can opener, pliers, screwdriver, nail file, and collapsible Batman Batarang), my belt was no match for the gravitational pull of my pants.

I was horrified, but not half as horrified as when I learned that Tosca's assistant had filmed the entire episode with her iPhone. It just so happened that that very week, the new Facebook Live feature was introduced. As a result, the video of me losing my shorts rocketed into the digital universe, exploding on social media.

Before the night was over, the video had amassed more than 50,000 views. Conference attendees discovered the video and began sharing it with all the gusto of early church evangelists sharing the Good News. If only we took the Great Commission this seriously.

For the first half hour after the video streamed on Facebook, I tried my best to act like I thought it was funny. I'd rather be in on the joke than the butt of the joke. I continued to put on this good-sport act as they showed the video at the ICVM awards for anyone who happened to miss it, and then they gifted me with a pair of suspenders. Which I promptly stuffed into my apocalypse pocket. Because ya just never know.

• • • • • • • • •

In the end, I learned that pride is not a part of my calling, but it is a part of my struggle. God wants me to walk in obedience to my calling, but He wants me to do it humbly. And if I don't humble myself, He has no problem doing it for me. Whenever I'm tempted to show off that I'm friends with an award-winning New York Times bestselling author (which I am!), my ego is ripe to be popped. God will use my ego as His piñata, busting apart my pretensions with one swift swing of His stick.

Sometimes I feel like I'm walking proof that God has a sense of humor and I'm His favorite punch line. When my pride went to my head, my cargo shorts fell to my ankles, proving that old saying true: "Pride goeth before the fall."

TOSCA LEE AND TORRY DE. This is proof that I'm good friends with New York Times bestselling author Tosca Lee. (I know you were hoping to see a photo of my falling shorts, but for that you'll have to check out the YouTube video on my website—www. torrymartin.com.)

19
LIGHT MY FIRE

"Please, Father, let my wallet be stolen," I prayed in my hotel room in Amsterdam. "Bring forth the pickpocket that You would most like to be rewarded. I put my wallet into Your hands, Lord, and I ask that You will place it into theirs."

For most people, having their wallet stolen while on a European vacation would be a nightmare. But for me it would be a dream come true.

I was in Amsterdam for the Christian European Visual Media Association Conference, and I planned a side trip to Dublin on the way home. With my red hair and Irish descent, I had always wanted to go to Ireland. After all, I had recently been compared to an Irish sumo wrestler and the Lucky Charms mascot with gout, so I felt it was my sacred duty.

Prior to leaving, some of my Facebook friends had warned me all about the pickpockets in Europe. "If you take the hop-on, hop-off bus tour in Ireland, you've got to be especially careful because it's also known as the pickpocket express," said one friend.

"The trains in Amsterdam aren't much better," said another. "Make sure you keep your wallet in your front pocket."

A third Facebook friend added, "Some Gypsies work in teams and use their kids as distractions to gain your trust. They'll charm the wallet right out of your pants."

A week before my trip, I was at Goodwill and happened to spot a table full of old wallets, which caused me to remember the pickpocket warnings and triggered an idea. *If I'm going to get pickpocketed, I might as well have some fun with it.* So I bought five of them and put together what I called my Witness Wallets.

I loaded the wallets with Christian tracts and had ten euros sticking out of them to lure pickpockets. I also added my business card with a different Bible verse written on each one. Then, in the plastic window of the wallet, where a driver's license normally appears, I inserted a card that said: "Congratulations! You have stolen a Witness Wallet!"

On my first day in Amsterdam, however, I failed to attract a single pickpocket, but that wasn't God's fault. For that I blame my pants. They were new and a little too tight. If a pickpocket tried to slip a hand into my back pocket, he'd never be able to pull it out. My pockets were the Chinese finger traps of trousers.

The next day I put on my bush pants. These pants were bigger and baggier, with multiple pockets. In fact, these pants were almost too baggy. My wallet was buried so far down in the large pockets that any would-be thief would have to stick his entire arm into it. I solved this problem by packing the bottom of my back pocket with some wadded-up tissues and slipping the wallet on top. That way my wallet rode higher and would even stick out a little. If a pickpocket saw me, I would be a walking, five-fingered temptation.

The tissues worked—I had two wallets stolen in Amsterdam, which left me with three for Ireland. Getting pickpocketed was thrilling. Seriously, I got an adrenaline rush every time. I was especially excited the day I got set on fire. That was very cool. It was also very, very warm—but overall...cool.

I had just finished shopping, and I was standing at the hop-on, hop-off bus stop with about 25 people when I suddenly felt a fierce tugging on my shirt, and I looked down to see a short woman in Gypsy clothes, saying in broken English, "Umm... This! This!" She was pointing to the shopping bag in my right hand.

I quickly realized what "this" was. My 100 percent cotton bag was 100 percent on fire! My newly purchased souvenirs were about to go up in smoke.

The fire appeared to have started in the center of the bag, and it was flaring out to all sides. As I frantically patted the bag, the fire singed my finger, forcing me to drop the bag to the ground. Then I tapped down the flames with my foot.

During all of this commotion, I thought I felt a slight tug coming from the back pocket of my pants, but I wasn't sure. I was too busy putting out the fire to look. After I finally extinguished my badly burned bag, I reached back to check on my wallet and discovered that it was gone—and so was the Gypsy woman who had told me my bag was on fire.

An elderly Irishman sitting on a nearby bench hopped up and hurried to my side.

"I saw the whole thing! That Gypsy woman held her cigarette 'gainst yer bag until it lit," he said. "The next thing I know, I saw the flames and her pointin' 'em out to you! And when ya was putting it out, her partner pinched your wallet, and they took off that way." He pointed toward Saint Patrick's Cathedral. "I saw it with my own eyes, I did! 'Twas unbelievable!"

As he was telling me this, I couldn't help but chuckle. The two thieves had probably taken one look at my size and picked me as their victim, thinking I was the only one they were certain they could outrun. I like to picture them sprinting away, sitting down on the steps of Saint Patrick's Cathedral while excitedly digging into the wallet, only to discover the gospel message. There is just something ironic and romantic about imagining it that way.

"I shoulda done somethin'," the bystander said, obviously embarrassed. "But it happened so fast I could'na think!"

"Don't worry about it. I've still got my real wallet right here," I said, patting the right front pocket of my bush pants. "They just stole my Witness Wallet."

"Your what?"

"Witness Wallet. I *wanted* it to get stolen."

When I explained what I had done, it was now the Irish fellow's turn to break out laughing. "That's deadly news!" he exclaimed. "Brilliant!" Then he turned to another fellow and said, "Didja hear that? They pinched his wallet, but he went arseways with the gospel on 'em."

Arseways with the gospel? That's got to be the funniest line I've ever heard!

"Arseways" is Irish slang that means to totally mess things up. In other words, "He went arseways with the gospel" means I had fouled up the thieves' plan by luring them into pinching my wallet and giving them the gospel instead.

The pickpockets had stolen my wallet, but I wanted the Word of God to steal into their hearts. Even though I had been set on fire, my burning desire was to show God's pure love to the cash-stealing couple.

• • • • • • • • •

During the agony of the crucifixion, Jesus told one of the two thieves hanging next to Him, "Today you will be with me in paradise" (Luke 23:43). So I prayed that my two thieves would likewise turn their lives around and someday join Him there too.

Whatever our mission in life, whatever our calling may be, we need to remember that it's not about us—it's about others. Our main calling is to lift up the name of Jesus, even if our wallets get lifted in the process.

Another way I tried to be creative in my calling while in Ireland was by teaming up with Molly Malone. I met her outside Saint Andrew's Church at the top of Suffolk Street. She was a looker but not very talkative. Probably because she was a statue.

Molly Malone was a fictional character—the heroine of a song that has become the unofficial anthem of Dublin. The song tells the story of Molly, a poor fishmonger who dies of a fever. The famous statue shows her in a seventeenth-century dress that, shall we say, emphasizes Molly's bosomy physique. Think of her as Molly Parton—Dolly's Irish cousin.

Being a modest American evangelical, I figured that if I placed my Bible-verse business cards in Molly's ample cleavage, they'd cover her up and make her a bit more respectable to viewers. Plus, it was a much more likely place for my business cards to catch the public's eye. It took 14 cards to fill that enormous gap, which rivaled Ireland's famous Cliffs of Moher.

People watched with great interest as I scribbled Bible verses on business card after business card and carefully placed them in Molly's "business card holder."

So what was the verse on the business cards being held in the bust of my Bible-thumping bosom buddy? That's easy.

Deuteronomy 11:22 (KJV): "Cleave unto him."

WITNESS WALLET. As a fisher of men, you've got to be prepared to let people fish in your pocket.

BURNING MAN. This is the bag the Gypsy lit with her cigarette just before I went arseways with the gospel on them. (When people say smoking is dangerous, I'm not sure this is what they have in mind.)

20
FROM RUSSIA WITH LOVE

She was leaning against the door of the motel entrance, trying to act nonchalant, when our eyes met. She appeared to be Russian with startling green eyes and silky, smooth hair. "Hi, beautiful," I said, being a little forward.

She looked at me coolly but didn't say a word. There was something in her eyes that made me uneasy. Knowing trouble when I saw it, I decided to ignore her and hurried to my room. I was just opening the door when I sensed I was being followed. I slowly turned around, and there she was, still giving me that look, saying everything with her eyes.

Determined to flee from temptation, I slipped into my room and locked the door behind me.

I thought I was safe until I heard a tapping against the window. Hesitating for a moment, I got up, pulled back the curtain slightly, and peeked out. Sure enough, there she was, mere inches from the window, staring in, giving me her best "come hither" look.

It was then that I made a *very* bad decision. I opened the door and let her in.

Stupid cat.

I'm a sucker when it comes to strays, probably because I see myself in them. This stray was a Russian blue, and unlike most feral cats, she appeared to be completely unafraid of humans.

After petting her for a few minutes, I put her back outside my room and walked around the building to the hotel office.

"Is that cat yours?" I asked the woman in charge.

"No, it belonged to a young couple who stayed here about a month ago," she explained. "But I could tell the boyfriend didn't care for cats."

When the couple checked out, the boyfriend loaded everything into the back hatch of their car, including the cat, which was curled up in a small pet carrier. But at the last second, with the girlfriend in the front seat and completely oblivious, the boyfriend stealthily pulled the cat out of the carrier and left the poor kitten in the parking lot. Then he hopped into the car and sped off with his girlfriend, who was still unaware that he had let her cat out of the bag.

I can't help but hope that after the girl discovered her cat was missing that she not-so-stealthily opened the door and pushed her boyfriend out, leaving him in a parking lot in the middle of nowhere before speeding off.

"You can have the cat if you want," the motel manager told me. "She's beautiful and deserves a good home."

That was true. She was one of the most beautiful cats I'd ever seen, and my heart broke knowing that she was separated from her owner. We already had four cats, but in the end, I couldn't resist a stray. The friendly and affectionate cat stayed in my room all night, and by the next morning there was no way I could leave her behind.

"I'll take her," I told the motel manager when I was checking out.

The manager was thrilled. "God bless you, sir. May His blessing come back to you threefold!"

However, after getting the cat to her new home in Tennessee, it was her scorn that came back to me threefold. She went from being the sweetest, kindest, gentlest creature to being a loud, feisty hisser. She hated our dogs. She hated our other cats. She hated being held. In short, she hated everything. My Russian blue had become Josephine

Stalin, the demon commie cat. Rob decided to name her Sky, but I still think a better name might have been "Benito Meowssolini" because of how she treated everyone.

About two weeks later, I was on the road again, teaching at another writer's conference, when Rob called to report the latest development.

"I think Sky's pregnant," he said.

"She can't be pregnant. She's only seven or eight months old."

"Well, her stomach has tripled in size this week."

"She's eating regularly now. She's bound to gain weight," I explained.

"No, her nipples are getting kinda big too."

"She's probably storing food there."

Rob dismissed me with his favorite word: "Whatever." (By the way, according to a recent Marist Poll of 1,005 individuals, the word "whatever" was voted the most annoying word or phrase for the eighth year in a row. I had no idea Rob even knew that many people!)

Still, there was no way Sky could be pregnant. We'd only had her for a couple of weeks, and she hadn't been out of the house once. And all of our other pets were fixed.

When I got home from my trip, I inspected Sky, and while she did look chubbier, I wasn't convinced she was pregnant. There was no way to really tell unless...

I jumped in my car and drove down to the Dollar General and bought an 88-cent pregnancy test. But when I returned home with the kit, I realized I hadn't fully thought it through.

How am I going to get Sky to pee on a pregnancy stick? Do I leave the pee stick in the litter box and hope she strikes it by accident? No, that's too much like playing Russian roulette. Maybe I'll just give her a lot of water and make her watch a Friday the 13th *marathon and hope it scares the pee out of her. Or I could place her in a long line at the DMV. That's when I always need to go. Hmm...there has to be a better way...*

That's how I wound up dangling Sky by the scruff of her neck over the toilet while simultaneously holding the pregnancy stick underneath her.

"Go ahead, Sky. You can do it."

Nothing. *She must have a shy bladder.* I allowed her some privacy by turning my head away, and I gave her two gentle shakes to get her started.

RAAAWWWRRR!

Screaming! Clawing! Her razor-sharp claws scratched the back of my hand.

"AAAHHH!"

Now we were both yowling. Sky dropped out of my hands, and the pregnancy stick fell into the toilet. She ran to safety while I ran for the first-aid kit, worried that this pregnancy scare would become a pregnancy scar.

I was in the kitchen wrapping a paper towel around my hand when Rob came home.

"What happened to you?" he asked.

"Nothing."

Rob shrugged, and his eyes drifted to the counter, where he spotted the empty box for the pregnancy test.

"Who's that for?"

"Sky."

Rob just stared at me blankly.

"I wanted to find out if she was pregnant," I said.

"So you used a *human* pregnancy kit? Those don't work on cats."

"I know. Cats won't pee no matter how hard you shake them over the toilet. I think they're afraid of pregnancy results."

"Or they're afraid of water," Rob said dryly.

"Oh."

To me, I was just holding her over a toilet, but to Sky I was threatening to drown her in Lake Superior. I feel like an idiot now. If I were smarter, I would have shaken her over the litter box.

· · · · · · · · · ·

Perspective is everything.

If we look at things from God's perspective, we can see that He has a plan whenever He calls us into a fearful place. He's not just dangling us over water to scare us. When everything around us seems terrifying, we can get through it if we just trust that we're in God's hands.

So the next time you feel like you're being dangled over the toilet bowl of life, don't look down. Look up.

ROB: That's not a picture of Sky.

TORRY: I know. It's a random cat I met in Homer, Alaska, but it's the best selfie I've ever taken, and I had a spot for another picture.

ROB: So you're just sneaking in this photo for vanity's sake?

TORRY: I know. I'm good, right? *(Pause)* Besides, it's me with a cat, so it relates.

ROB: Whatever.

21
REVELATIONS

I'd like to interrupt this book to get real for a second.

I want you to know me better and to also lower your expectations of me so I can live up to them—or down to them, whatever the case may be. That's why I'd like to use this chapter to tell you some things about myself. Things that very few people know. *Ooo...intrigue.*

If you scare easily, you should probably skip on to chapter 22. (You should also avoid the book of Revelation.) Otherwise, brace yourself for an odd journey into the mind, habits, and nature of Torry Martin.

1. I talk to myself a lot. And if you combine that with my ADHD, the discussions can get complicated. I'll be in the middle of a conversation with myself and get lost, and then I have to ask, "What were we just talking about? I know you know, because you're me. Tell me!" And for the record, talking to yourself is actually indicative of high intelligence. (At least that's what I tell myself.)

2. My superpower is shopping. I call myself "Captain Clearance," and Rob is my archnemesis—the Meddler of Moola (or M.O.M. for short). He's the kind of archnemesis that gets on your nerves at times but actually saves you from yourself.

3. I like being single. If it was good enough for Mother Teresa, the

apostle Paul, and the professor on *Gilligan's Island*, it's good enough for me. I actually feel called to be single. Besides, I share my bed with my dog, and not many women are comfortable sleeping on the floor.

4. When someone asks me for my honest opinion on something, that's what they'll get. I'm not good at editing my thoughts on the fly. If you're going to ask me what I think and you want an immediate answer, you should probably be wearing protective clothing.

5. I hide things when I think I'm going to get into trouble. Once, Rob laid down the law and said, "As your financial manager, I cannot allow you to go into another store of any kind and buy one more thing." But I secretly continued to buy my favorite pairs of shoes online (Doc Martens). When it came time to move from our home, we had to stop the U-Haul at our neighbor's house to pick up the 37 pairs that I had secretly stored there. A forest fire of smoke came out of Rob's ears, and I had to grab one of my 26 pairs of Converse All Stars to outrun him.

By the way, Rob became my financial adviser after I declared bankruptcy 24 years ago. It's no secret I can't do math, so I guess it was inevitable. I'm still on an allowance that's so tight it makes me long for the one I had in junior high. That's why I excel in sneakiness.

6. Occasionally I get frustrated with God. Sometimes I think it would be easier to serve Him from an advisory position. (Oh, don't act like you've never had the same thought. We're human!)

7. I hate air dryers in public bathrooms. I require paper towels. The door handle on the inside of a public bathroom is the Grand Central Station of germs. So if there aren't any paper towels for me to use to open the door, I will wait inside until someone comes in and then scoot through the open door so I don't have to touch it. If Rob ever notices I'm suddenly missing at Walmart, he always knows where to find me. I'm trapped in the bathroom.

8. I like direct communication. Walking on eggshells with people is so tedious and time consuming. I'd much rather roller-skate on eggshells instead. It's a much more fun and expedient way to resolve

a conflict. It also helps me get out of the room faster should anything go awry.

9. I have nine pairs of electronic nose-hair clippers. Don't ask.

10. My silverware drawer is insanely pristine. I can't control the things that happen to me in life, but that silverware drawer is the one thing I have complete mastery over. It gives me peace just to look at it. Every knife blade faces the same direction. In fact, whenever Rob wants me to make him something for dinner and I'm busy, all he has to do is go into the kitchen and start opening that drawer and slamming it shut over and over. He knows I'll come running to save my utensils from dishevelment.

11. I struggle. With everything. With writing, with acting, with overeating, with social anxiety, and with envy because it always feels like the Christian walk is a struggle for me and so easy for others.

12. I think all cats are liars. If they were really as clean as they claim to be, they'd empty their own litter boxes.

13. I buy on impulse a lot. Whenever we're going through the checkout line at the store, Rob hands me a watermelon or head of lettuce or anything and says, "Hold this." Then he goes back to checking out. He doesn't need me to hold it—he just wants to keep my hands occupied so I don't buy more fingernail clippers. I already have 60.

14. Sometimes I round down to make myself look less neurotic. I actually have 72 fingernail clippers. (I purchased all 72 on Amazon for the amazing price of $19.99.)

14a. I like a deal.

15. I talk with my hands a lot. Rob calls it "propeller arms." He once said that what I lack in vocabulary I more than make up for with excessive facial expressions and hand gestures. Of course, I dismissed his comment with a wave of my arm and a roll of my eyes.

16. Stress is the one thing I'm not good at. Well, that and sports, and anything mechanical or electrical or requiring math ability or...Okay, forget it. Stress is the one thing I *am* good at.

17. I cushion things. If I'm ever going to confess to a big thing, I'll

confess to 17 smaller things and then the big thing, and then I'll follow it up with a few more small things, hoping that the big thing will
get lost in the shuffle.

18. The trip to Africa was one of the most stressful times of my life.
In fact, that was the place where I started smoking cigarettes again
after nine years of being nicotine-free. I'm sure some of you just threw
this book across the room in disgust. That's okay. I'll sit right here and
wait for you to pick it back up. Take your time. I'll just grab a smoke.

. . . .

I honestly don't blame you if you're disappointed in me for smoking. I'm disappointed in myself. It's a struggle I deal with every day. I
debated whether to put this in the book, but I wanted to be real. Also,
some of you might be struggling with something in your past that you
thought you conquered, and you feel ashamed. I want you to know I
get it. And you're not alone. The struggle is real.

Fulfilling your calling often means admitting your weaknesses
(like smoking) and confessing your sins (like envy) so that you can
begin to heal and move past them, and so that the barrier that hurts
relationships is gone and you can concentrate on doing God's work.

James 5:16 says, "Confess your sins to each other and pray for each
other so that you may be healed." I often want to confess when I'm
struggling, but the fear of what others think of me is more power-
ful. Yet how can the body of Christ grow when we're not praying for
each other to overcome our weaknesses? And how will our brothers
in Christ know our weaknesses if we don't feel comfortable sharing
them? The mutual preference for frankness over flattery is what leads
to iron sharpening iron.

A Christian organization once offered me a job, but before I
accepted it, I thought they should know that I smoked because I didn't
feel right about hiding it. They immediately rescinded the job offer. I
don't really blame them for taking that stand, but it certainly has made
me more hesitant to be transparent with other Christians.

It shouldn't be that way. The church is the place where we're supposed to be able to go when we don't have it all figured out. Jesus came for the sick and the lost. The pressure to be perfect is the inhibitor to being real.

When it comes right down to it, I'd rather be real and rejected than fake and accepted. Because when I'm real, I can live with myself. Being fake affects my faith.

I'd like to confess more of my faults, but my publishers gave me a 60,000-word limit. So let's wrap this up and continue the shuffle so maybe you'll forget that I smoke.

19. I hate word-count limits, no matter if they're words in print or words coming out of my mouth. Rob told me that when I'm talking to someone, the absolute stopping point is three a.m. That is *so* restricting! What if I'm in the middle of a great story about my childhood trip to Sea World at two fifty-nine? I find the idea of someone limiting my word length to express myself personally offensive.

20. I complain a lot. Usually about word limits.

Anyway, I'm done talking about how bad I am. I'd appreciate your prayers for the areas where I struggle, especially the smoking. Cigarettes are almost six dollars a pack, so for the sake of my allowance, I'm begging you—pray! (In the meantime, can someone please pass me the ashtray?)

22

SHEAR PAIN

It had been a year since my return from Africa, and I was still struggling spiritually. I felt separated from God, and I wasn't sure how to make that right. I didn't know where to start. I felt as if my prayers were hitting the ceiling and bouncing into the recycle bin, only to be sent up again later.

I didn't feel like myself—I didn't feel like cleaning, cooking, or even shopping (*gasp!*). That's when you know things are bad. The last thing I wanted to do was pack, but that's exactly what I had to do. I was supposed to go to Pennsylvania for the Montrose Christian Writers Conference, where I was scheduled to teach a few classes and give a keynote address.

Packing for these trips is usually fun, but in my currently unhappy state of mind, I was less enthusiastic about doing it. I was going to have to call on Julie Andrews, or more specifically, Maria from *The Sound of Music*.

MARIA: Whenever something bothers me and I'm feeling unhappy, I try to think of nice things.

TORRY: What kind of nice things?

MARIA: Well, let me see...nice things...daffodils!

TORRY: I'm allergic.

MARIA: Green meadows?

TORRY: Chiggers.

MARIA: Skies full of stars?

TORRY: Nearsighted.

MARIA: Raindrops on roses?

TORRY: Those aren't raindrops. That was my dog.

MARIA: You know, I've always found that misery is made more tolerable when you set it to a catchy tune, like "My Favorite Things."

TORRY: That's perfect.

MARIA: Feel free to use the tune. The lyrics are copyrighted.

Cue the music.

MY TRAVELING THINGS

It's hard to pack when I don't know the weather.
It might get cold, so bring vests and a sweater.
Twelve pairs of shorts just in case it gets hot.
Toss in all nine brands of sunscreen I bought.

Solid and printed on flannel and cotton.
Pack everything that I think I look hot in.
Take 20 briefs and some plaid boxers too.
Ten pairs of Levis will just have to do.

I never know when my pants will surrender.
Better bring belts and three pairs of suspenders.
Boots, shoes, and sandals with socks that all match,
Look at my suitcase, it's packed to the max.

Use your man-might!
Zip those bags tight!
Somehow jam it in.

And when I'm preparing for my return flight,
Then I'll do it aaall again.

Arriving at the Montrose conference safely was easy, but unpacking my car safely? Not so much. I was just pulling the biggest piece of luggage out of the backseat when I threw my back out. I immediately regretted putting the emergency anvil in there. (You never know when you're going to need to forge something. And right then, I needed to forge a back brace.)

I was in so much pain, I could barely move. The entire week, it took me four times as long to get where I had to go. On the first day, I was late for the class I was teaching, but I blame heavy traffic on the conference grounds. I was shuffling so slowly through the garden that I had to pull over to let a snail and two slugs pass.

I avoided any kind of extra movement. If I needed a pen to write something down and the pen was two inches beyond my reach, I decided it wasn't important enough to write down. A single stair was Mount Everest. (There were 12 stairs to the cafeteria, but strangely enough I never missed a meal.)

Just putting my socks on made me feel like a kamikaze pilot making a death dive to the floor. I went on Facebook and asked for prayer for both myself and for the students in my classes. I figured they'd need healing too when they saw that the only thing I could manage to put on were my socks.

I had some time before my keynote address, and all I wanted to do was lie down on my bed and give my aching back a rest. But I couldn't for two reasons. First, my hair was *banging* that day! I couldn't risk mussing my mane attraction before the address. Second, I was concerned that if I lay down, I didn't think I'd ever be able to get back up. I might end up like one of those injured mountain climbers who have to be helicoptered out. With no other option, I leaned against the corner of my hotel room wall and stood for 60 minutes, staring at my bed like it was a chocolate donut.

That evening I delivered my keynote address without a hitch despite the excessive pain. Afterward a friend gave me a book called *A Shepherd Looks at Psalm 23* by Phillip Keller. After shuffling back to my room, I lay down on my bed to read it.

My friend had no idea how appropriate this book was. It talks about the relationship between sheep and their shepherd. Most people know that sheep are pretty dumb animals and need someone to look out for them at all times. They are in danger of wandering off alone, falling off a cliff, or ending up too close to predators. Sheep are also vulnerable to another danger that is completely self-inflicted.

Sheep can easily become "cast down." According to Keller, this is an old English term shepherds used when sheep toppled over on their back and couldn't get up again by themselves.

The sheep most vulnerable to being cast down are the fat ones who look for comfortable, soft spots on the ground to lie down. (Heavy people require more padding.) It's those soft spots that make it so easy for them to roll onto their backs. A sheep may roll onto its side slightly to stretch or relax. Suddenly the center of gravity in the body shifts, and it rolls over so far that its feet no longer touch the ground. With no traction, the sheep panics, and its flailing makes things even worse. It rolls over even farther. Now its feet are straight up in the air, and the sheep is completely unable to turn upright without help.

When a sheep winds up on its back, gases build in its rumen and can cut off circulation to the legs. A cast sheep can die in this position in only a few hours if it doesn't get help. Meanwhile, vultures begin to circle when they notice an incapacitated sheep on its back because they know the end is near. If the shepherd doesn't come soon, it's lamb chops for dinner.

You can probably already hear the metaphor machine revving up. What a picture of us—or more specifically, me. I was spiritually and physically flat on my back. This wasn't the first time I found myself in this predicament, but it was definitely the worst. In the past, I have relied heavily on God to rescue me, and He never gets tired of doing so, even when I make the same mistakes over and over again. But this time, no matter how loudly I cried for help, He didn't seem to be responding. I was just a fat sheep flailing.

Interestingly enough, the well-fed, content, and perhaps lazy sheep are the ones the shepherd has to rescue most often. Therefore, a shepherd who moves his sheep to more difficult terrain is actually protecting them from soft spots where they might get cast down.

The Good Shepherd does the same thing with us. He moves us into less comfortable pastures to make us stronger. When I think of it that way, I get less frustrated with God for allowing me to be uncomfortable. It could very well be for my own good, but that doesn't mean I like it.

And then there's the issue of too much wool. If the fleece gets too long, it becomes matted with mud, manure, burrs, and all sorts of other junk that weighs it down. In the same way, getting matted down with the junk of life can cause us to get cast flat on our backs. I need the Father to regularly trim me back a little bit—cut off the wool that's weighing me down. For me, getting sheared is terrifying, and not just because I have great hair.

Sometimes God has to take stuff away from me, or I'd hold on to it forever until I ended up flat on my back, covered in muck and manure and vulnerable to the vultures' attack. As much as it hurts, I have to let God take away the things that are going to hurt me in the end. John 15:2 says, "He cuts off every branch in me that bears no fruit, while every branch that does bear fruit he prunes so that it will be even more fruitful."

The pruning is awful, but the fruit is delicious.

For us sheep, the wool will grow back after we're sheared. But if we're not careful, it will become matted again, requiring more cutting. Probably sooner than we'd like.

The Christian writer's conference showed my movie *Heaven Bound*, and I stood in the back, uncomfortably, to watch the reaction of the audience. They laughed at all the funny parts and reacted appropriately to the more touching scenes. People were watching a movie that I cowrote, coproduced, and starred in. You'd think I'd be enjoying it. Professionally, it was a fulfillment of every area of my calling, but personally, I was spiritually far from God, and a lot of junk was weighing me down. I was definitely *not* enjoying it.

I had a lot of burrs in my wool, and a couple of them came from the industry I'm in. As much as I don't want to admit this, the Christian entertainment industry is a business just like any other. It would be nice to be able to say that people put the ministry first, but anyone with their eyes open would have to admit that this is frequently not the case. It's often about money. That's not necessarily a bad thing. People have to earn a living. But no one ever stabs a Christian brother in the back for the purpose of ministry. It's the insatiable craving to advance their career that causes this.

I remember talking to Rob about a painful betrayal by another believer. Someone had presented himself as a friend but was really just using me to make connections in the industry and advance his own career, even at the cost of mine. When I confronted him about his actions, he said, "It's called 'show business,' not 'show friendship.' That's the way of the world, brother."

"Exactly," I replied. "It's the way of the world. It's not the way of a 'brother'...brother."

This hurt went deep because I had invested a lot in the friendship. But I had once again discovered the sad reality that Christians will backbite other believers just to get a job—or make an inside connection. And I have the teeth marks to prove it. There's blood in the water, and it ain't the blood of Jesus.

I felt stupid for being so trusting, and it jaded me more than a little. It was hard for Rob to see this happen. When all you can do is watch things play out for someone, it is often just as painful for the observer as it is the participant. Rob was fed up.

"I understand you're hurt, but you're allowing it to change you," he said. "It's wise to guard your heart, but don't insulate it."

"But keeping a hard lesson from creating a hard heart is hard work," I said. "And I'm tired of being taken advantage of."

Rob had stopped paying attention to me midway through my last sentence. He was looking around the room, under the couch and beneath pillows.

"What are you looking for?" I asked.

"Your big boy pants," he said.

"*What?*"

"You need to start thinking of this guy as just a random accident. Like you're driving down the highway with your eternal destination in mind and you see a car crash. You acknowledge the accident, but you don't keep your eyes on the wreckage as you continue down the road. You don't glue your eyes to the rearview mirror or turn your head to watch it fade in the distance. Because if you do that, your eyes won't be on the road in front of you and you'll drive straight off a cliff. Just acknowledge the 'accident,' use the lesson to make you a better driver, and keep your eyes on the road."

I tried to do what Rob said by keeping my eyes on the road ahead, but I was still miserable. However, as we've already learned, misery is made more tolerable when you set it to a catchy tune. And once again, I'll use "My Favorite Things."

Hit it, maestro!

MY INDUSTRY STINGS

He seemed trustworthy and came recommended.
Turns out he wasn't and had just pretended.
Look at this contract in good faith I signed.
What was I thinking? I must have been blind.

New friends and good deals with promises spoken.
Both are now gone, and their word has been broken.

Covered in bruises with cuts that run deep,
Never do business with wolves dressed as sheep.

Stabbed in the back by someone I befriended.
Contracts looked good until they got amended.
Lied through his teeth with his motives impure.
How much manure can one man endure?

When the sharks bite!
That's just show biz!
Sometimes you get had.
Just simply remember that vengeance is His
And then you won't feel so mad.

While the industry I'm in frequently makes me sad, it's also where I met Marshal Younger, who has been my writing partner and second-best friend for 15 years. It's also where I met my friend Doug Peterson, who wrote this book with me. There are so many more I could name—all people who have my back.

Speaking of which, my friends at Montrose also had my back, literally. When I posted on Facebook about my back problems, I received an overwhelming response. Prayers flooded my way, and advice came from all over the country. People at the conference inundated me with painkillers, rubs, lotions, essential oils (actually it was the essential oils that allowed me to slip into my skinny jeans—well, *skinnier* jeans; they were a size too small), prescription meds, stretching exercises, natural remedies, unnatural remedies, and several offers of impromptu back massages from people I barely knew.

These people were worried about me. (And to be honest, I was worried about some of them. Giving a back massage to a stranger in a lobby is just weird.) They cared and they prayed. And it's always the caring people who keep me going in this job. The good people greatly outnumber the bad. I'm in this industry because I love it, and I'm thankful for every job I've ever gotten. There are times, however, when I wish it was done better. We can be good to each other and make good products at the same time. For me, the projects come and go. It's the friendships that last.

After Montrose, it was clear. I was in need of a serious shearing and a spiritual rebirth. For that, I needed to get away from it all as far as I could. My last hope was the Last Frontier: Alaska.

23

FROM HERE TO MATERNITY

I am about to say the most difficult words in the English language: *Rob was right.*

Our new cat, Sky, was indeed pregnant, and it must have happened at the motel. Turns out that our house-cat hisser was a hotel hussy.

Sky had been abandoned as a kitten, so it fell entirely upon me to prepare her with neonatal lessons. But to quote the feline version of *Gone with the Wind*, "I don't know nuthin' 'bout birthin' no kittens!" I became as obsessed as a first-time father preparing for the arrival of his child, but I needed some help from my Facebook friends. I posted a picture of Sky sitting with a sour expression in front of six different types of pickles. My caption read, "Sky is picky about pickles, and I'm at a loss. What type of pickles does a pregnant cat crave?" (Ooo! A new tongue twister!)

The response was immediate, and so was the mocking. After several people pointed out that cats don't eat pickles, one helpful person said they do eat umbilical cords. "I had to tie the cords off with dental floss as she [the cat, I hope] couldn't bite through them herself...so be prepared for that part also."

Now I have to worry about umbilical cords? Not gonna happen. I

decided I'd make sure Sky could chew through the cords by strength-
ening her jaw muscles. If there was anything I could teach this cat, it
was how to chew. At that, I'm an expert.

But how was I going to teach a cat to chew through an umbilical cord? This was going to take some ingenuity. Next destination:
Walmart, where I bought six stuffed toy kittens and a package of pepperoni sticks. Then I carefully cut a slit into each stuffed kitten and
inserted a pepperoni—my fake umbilical cord. When I set them in
front of Sky, my pregnant cat devoured them with gusto, demonstrating that her jaw muscles were working just fine. Scratch that one
off my list—but she still had a lot more to learn before I left on my
upcoming trip back to Alaska.

Lesson number two: nursing.

Sky looked at me quizzically as I stood before her in my Cowardly
Lion costume. I thought Sky would learn a lot faster if I looked like
a cat.

For this demonstration, I pinned the six stuffed kittens to the chest
of my lion costume to simulate nursing, and then I gulped down a big
glass of milk to show Sky what the kittens were doing. Her only reaction was to spit up a hairball. Either she was congested or nauseated
by my teaching methods.

Lesson number three: labor and delivery.

Still in my lion costume, I stretched out on the couch, placed all six
stuffed kittens behind me, raised a leg, and tossed the kittens toward
Sky, one at a time.

"You never know when labor is going to happen," I cautioned her.
"When you least expect it, BOOM!"

I winged another one of the kittens through my legs and across
the room, bonking Sky right on the noggin, firmly planting this lesson deep in her brain.

Lesson number four: birthing boxes.

As the big day neared, Sky became obsessed with finding a proper
birthing spot, which meant that I became obsessed with it too.

I had some collapsible organization boxes from IKEA, so I decided to use one of them for Sky to give birth in. I lined it with a towel (because birth is messy), and I read that I should include something that carried my scent. So I grabbed a T-shirt out of the dirty laundry and slipped it beneath the towel.

The final touch was to line the inside walls of the box with eight-by-ten promotional photos of myself. I was afraid I'd be in Alaska when Sky gave birth, and I wanted my face to be the first thing the kittens saw so our bonding could begin. I chose the photo where I was acting coy but approachable.

I had constructed the perfect birthing box, but then Sky promptly moved to a completely different nesting site—as far away from that birthing box as she could get. I wasn't going to let that stop me, so I built a second birthing box at the site she chose, complete with towel, Torry T-shirt, and eight-by-ten glossies. She moved again.

I built a third box. And a fourth. After 11 of them, I had run out of boxes.

But then one of my Facebook friends pointed out that their cat had given birth on their bed. Just in case that happened, I used packing tape to attach my eight-by-ten glossies to the sides of my bed so that the pictures faced inward and showed above the mattress on all sides. If Sky gave birth on my bed, she would be completely surrounded by my coy but approachable face.

When Rob peeked into my bedroom to see what I was doing, he slowly backed out, mumbled, "Whatever," and continued down the hall.

Lesson number five: labor and delivery, part 2.

My final step was to purchase all the supplies necessary to deliver these kittens. So of course I wisely headed to the nearest medical supply store, also known as Dollar General. I bought replacement milk, a syringe, and eyedroppers in case Sky had problems nursing and I needed to step in. I also knew you weren't supposed to touch kittens at all for the first few days, but I wanted to be ready in case of an emergency. I bought a pair of tongs, and I used a rubber band to attach a sponge to each tong, giving me makeshift forceps.

Dollar General didn't have filtered surgical masks, so I bought a snorkel instead. By wearing the snorkel during delivery, I wouldn't expose the kittens to any contaminants. I even bought Rob a snorkel, although the green one is mine because it matches my shoes. Keeping up the tradition of all new fathers, I also bought some cigars to smoke—mango and cherry flavored. (Smoking is bad for you, but fruit isn't, so I figured they'd cancel each other out.) However…do you smoke just one cigar for the full litter, or do you smoke one cigar for every individual kitten born? Clearly I had more research to do.

One of the many Facebook friends who continued to give me advice on my preparations said, "You might be in danger of overthinking this," which I believe makes her the first person in history ever to say I was using too much of my brain.

Sadly, Sky didn't give birth before I took off on my trip back to Alaska, so I left a long list of instructions for Rob on the fridge. He pulled it down and tossed the list to the side without even looking at it.

Whatever birthing box Sky used now was all up to the Lord, I thought. I was hoping, though, that God was preparing a supernatural "rebirthing box" for me in Alaska. I was also hoping I wouldn't have to chew through an umbilical cord when I got there.

Labor and Delivery. The labor wasn't hard, but my delivery was a little off when I bonked Sky with a stuffed kitten (the blurry object in midair).

PERPLEXED BY PICKLES. Whether they're pregnant or not, it turns out that cats don't like pickles. So I ended up eating them for her. (The mango habanero was luscious.)

HOME SCHOOLED. As a responsible pet owner, I felt obligated to provide Sky with a visual demonstration of the proper way to nurse kittens. No real kittens were harmed in the demonstration.

DON'T KNOW NOTHING 'BOUT BIRTHIN' NO KITTENS! My forceps are particularly creative, don't you think? Dr. Quinn, Medicine Woman, would be impressed.

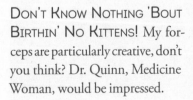

24
SOMETHING OLD, SOMETHING NEW

When my plane arrived in Anchorage, I stepped out and took a deep breath of fresh Alaskan air. *I'm home,* I thought.

I was surrounded by snowcapped mountains that were so majestic they made the Smoky Mountains look like the Smoky Molehills. The top half of the mountains were blanketed in light, and a shadow cut across their base, casting the bottom portion in dark blue tones, broken only by a green belt of trees. Crowning it all was a bright-blue summer sky.

I wasn't born in Alaska, but I think of it as my spiritual home. It's where I accepted the Lord and met my extended church family. It's the most important place on earth to me because it's where I've always felt closest to God. No distractions. Just mountains and rivers and wild animals that aren't baboons or pythons. I'm more of a moose and bear kind of guy. They don't drop from trees onto your head or slither up your pants. In Alaska you're on top of the world, so surely any prayers uttered here reach God faster than any spoken in the Lower 48. Plus, there's no smog to slow them down.

Officially I came to Alaska to film the places I had talked about in

my book *Of Moose and Men* and include them in a DVD of my comedy program. My unofficial reason for going to the Last Frontier was
to get away from distractions and focus completely on God. I wanted
to get back to the relationship I had with Him when I lived here. The
official reason allowed me to write off the trip, but the unofficial reason was far more important.

I traveled with Lucas Wilson, a filmmaker and a strong, young
man of God whom I had been mentoring. He was there to film the
bonus features.

You might think the first place I wanted to see upon returning to
Alaska was my cabin. But you'd be wrong. The first place I wanted
to see was the Anchorage Municipal Animal Control Center. Not
because it was so beautiful—in fact, if you took a deep breath of air
there, you'd instantly regret it. I wanted to start there because it's where
Rob and I received the biggest blessing from God we've ever had and
the best dog we've ever owned—Sam.

We now had three dogs in Tennessee, and they were amazing and
irreplaceable in their own way. But as much as I loved them, the three
of them combined didn't equal one Sam. Rob and I had been praying for more than a year that we would find another dog like Sam,
and I had an overwhelming sense that this new dog would come to
us around the time of my Alaska trip. So using Torry-logic, I thought
that this new dog would come from the same place where we found
Sam. Wouldn't that be ironic? Made sense to me.

Before entering the animal control center, Lucas and I prayed outside for God to help me choose the right dog. I also prayed that if I
was wrong, and there wasn't a dog here to be the new Sam, for God
to make it clear to me.

I posed confidently in front of the animal control center sign while
Lucas shot photos. I wanted the moment documented because I was
sure God had something in store for me. But when I stepped into
the place, something was wrong. I heard plenty of meowing but not
a single bark.

The center didn't have any dogs. Not even one. *God couldn't make it any clearer than that.*

"Where are all the dogs?" I asked the woman in charge. "Are they on a field trip to a dog spa? Playing poker in the basement?"

"No. People kinda like their dogs up here, so there aren't many strays being brought in," she said. "We had five dogs last week, but they were all gone by noon. We've got a lot of cats though, if you want to—"

"Nope, nope, nope. I've already got five cats, and one has kittens on the way. If I brought more home, I would officially be the cat man on our street. Little kids would point and laugh at me and meow in my direction, and I'd have to come out my front door and yell at them while wearing a fur-covered afghan. My life would change."

I was discouraged not to find the "Sam" dog we were praying for. I thought for sure I'd have him by the time I got home. I sent Rob a text to tell him that I struck out on the dog front and that I would text him some pictures when I got to the cabin. Rob hadn't seen the cabin in 20 years, and I wished he could've made the trip with me. We had had so many fond memories there I wanted to recapture—being knocked around by a reindeer in my kitchen, having a moose yank out my window frame with his antlers, accidentally shooting pepper spray in my face when I was aiming at a bear. Ah...home, sweet home.

Lucas and I passed the old sign that said, "Danger! Warning! 4-Wheel Drive Only! Chains Required! Enter at Your Own Risk!" It had to be the longest name of a street ever. Then we drove up the 200-yard driveway, which ended where the 175-yard trail leading up to the cabin began. But as we pulled up, I was surprised to see my old desk sitting at the trailhead, apparently about to be hauled off to the dump.

I'm a sentimental guy, and that desk was important to me. It was a heavy-duty steel desk that weighed a ton and had taken four of us to wrestle into the cabin. Rob had found the desk at a dump and brought it to the cabin as a surprise replacement for the broken cardboard table that I had been using to write at. This was the desk that held my first

computer that Rob gave to me. This was the desk on which I wrote
my first episode of *Adventures in Odyssey* and created the character of
Wooton Bassett. This was also the desk where I had written my first
book of comedy sketches. I called it my Desk of Inspiration, but now
my DOI was DOA and ready to be buried in the city dump.

I wanted to bring the desk back to Tennessee with me. But I figured
the baggage fee would be astronomical, and I probably wouldn't be
able to find anyone to help me jam it into the overhead compartment.

I headed up the trail to the cabin and noticed a new driveway to a
house I didn't remember being there. Apparently we had a neighbor.
His name was Matt, and he saw us and came over to introduce himself. I explained to him that we used to live in the cabin, and I asked
him if he had the number for Tom and Claire, the owners who had
let us live there. I wanted to get the key so I could go inside and look
around. Matt said he had their number at his place, so we followed
him back to get it. That's how we discovered his unique house. Matt
had built his entire home out of 150 solid wood doors from a hospital
in Alaska that was being demolished.

Random thoughts filled my mind.

How do you know how to get in?

Where do you put the doorbell?

This is one way to frustrate trick-or-treaters.

Your key chain must be enormous!

Lazy door-to-door salesmen would love this place.

Let me guess your favorite music group. Hmm…the Doors?

*Knock-knock jokes would be so much more complicated: "Knock,
knock." "Where are you?"*

As we left Matt's home, I called the owner of the cabin, and he told
us no one was living there at the moment and the door was unlocked,
so go right in. But even from a distance, I could see that the cabin
had fallen into disrepair. What was even more shocking was that I
could see the cabin from a distance! There was supposed to be a tree
in the middle of the deck that blocked the cabin from view. Rob had

carefully built the deck around the tree to preserve it. The tree had pro-truded through the deck, only three feet from the door, and I often ran into it on my way out. So I had placed a sign on the bark at eye level that said "TREE" with an arrow pointing up to keep myself from injury. But now the tree was gone. Someone had cut it down.

A lot of other trees had also been cleared to improve reception for the three enormous, ugly satellite dishes that had been installed on the left side of the cabin. *Satellite dishes? It's a cabin in the middle of the woods!* The whole idea was to escape civilization and hide away from the rush and tumble of everyday life. You don't build a cabin in the wil-derness to watch *The Walking Dead*! When you live here, you inten-tionally sacrifice your ability to keep up with the world. Heck, I didn't even find out about O.J. until the movie came out in 2016!

When I reached the cabin, I discovered a new knob on the outside door. I was amazed. That cabin hadn't had an outside doorknob for 20 years! We always just kicked the door open, which was convenient if your arms were full.

I entered, and as I wandered from room to room, soaking up the memories, I was shocked to find that the Incinolet toilet had been removed—a primitive toilet that incinerated its contents. *Where did it go? Is someone playing hide and seek with the toilet? Is this a new* Game of Thrones? I loved that toilet! I spent *many* productive hours there. In fact, I had signed my very first book contract on the lowered seat lid while Rob took the picture. (It wasn't a very good contract.)

Now, the Incinolet was gone. Stranger yet, it hadn't been replaced with anything else. *The cabin doesn't have a bathroom? That's one way to discourage squatters—and squatting.*

I also learned that there were plans to build a housing development right next to our once-isolated cabin. And another nearby homeowner was trying to get the cabin condemned!

So, to recap: (1) No dog, (2) no porch tree, and (3) no Incinolet toi-let (which meant no going 1 or 2). I had taken pictures of everything—the doorknob, the desk, the missing trees, and the missing toilet—and texted them to Rob. He texted me back: "Stop sending me pictures! You're destroying my memories! I don't even like the doorknob!"

Next, Lucas and I drove out to Bird Creek Campground, where Rob and I had served as camp hosts. We checked in people, maintained order, and—in my case—collected moose droppings for my moose-dropping jewelry. (I have a "How to Make a Moose-Dropping Christmas Garland" video on YouTube. Look it up. And yes, I take special orders.)

The most important place I wanted to see at the campground was the spot where I had first dedicated my life to Jesus. In fact, that was the most important part of my whole trip. That small dock was my spiritual birthing box. I planned to rededicate my life at the dock on the Turnagain Arm inlet near the Bird Creek Campground, so I had mentally prepared myself beforehand by smoking as many cigarettes as I could. I was determined to give them up and lay them down with the rest of my burdens.

As we pulled up to the Bird Creek Campground, I was confused and thought my memory must be faulty. *I don't remember it looking anything like this.* I soon discovered that the campground had been infested by beetles eight years earlier, killing all the trees in their path, and the Alaska Department of Natural Resources had to redesign the whole place.

I walked the trail to the small dock and found nothing there but water. *Did I go to the wrong spot?*

No. The dock was gone. This was the most devastating blow of all.

I had made a clear arrangement with God. He was supposed to meet me in Alaska, but He seemed to be saying, "No. I don't want to."

In my mind, the dock being gone meant I had nowhere to rededicate my life to God. *I suppose I could try walking out on the water, and if I succeed, I can probably assume that my rededication is a success.*

I lit a cigarette.

Sitting on a bench near the campground, my phone rang. It was Rob. "Sky had three kittens!"

"Three?"

I laughed, remembering the woman at the motel saying that I would receive a threefold blessing from God for adopting this stray cat. Sky had delivered one black boy kitten and two gray girls.

"Awesome! Which birthing box did she use?" I asked.

"None of 'em."

"What?"

"She had 'em in my underwear drawer," Rob said.

"What?"

"Sky had her kittens in *my* underwear drawer," he repeated smugly.

There was a pregnant pause (or in this case, a postpartum pause). I felt totally betrayed. *Sky didn't use any of the birthing boxes I so painstakingly prepared for her? That's crazy! They were IKEA!* It was the ultimate slap in my coy but approachable face. After I hung up, Rob texted me four pictures of the newborn kittens in his underwear drawer, just to rub my nose in it—and that's the last place I wanted my nose rubbed.

I immediately called him back, and what followed was the shortest phone call in history.

"Can you put a picture of me in your underwear drawer?" I asked.

"No."

CLICK!

Rob texted me another photo of the kittens in his underwear drawer. "Stop sending me pictures!" I texted him back.

After these letdowns, Lucas and I met for lunch with my pastor, Jack Aiken, and his wife, Ann. I'm an emotional eater, so I planned to order the whole menu.

I love my pastor and his wife and had been looking forward to talking with them. Jack had retired, and he told me that the congregation of our church had dwindled from 150 to about 50 people, and he said I probably wouldn't recognize many faces there because all the people I knew had moved on. I wasn't surprised. Alaska has such a high turnover rate, the state should issue double-sided license plates—one side for Alaska and the other side for the state you're heading to next.

I shared some of my discouragements, and they shared some of theirs. But mine didn't even compare. One week before I came to Alaska, Ann had been diagnosed with early-stage Parkinson's disease.

Despite Ann's health struggles, she and Jack hadn't changed when it came to their kindness, perseverance, wisdom, and faith. With them, I didn't have to put on the happy comic face. They were my spiritual mentors, and I needed some direction, encouragement, and to be honest, some sympathy. I lamented my string of heartbreaks, and after a long pause, Ann said something I will never forget.

"Our lives are a series of assignments given to us by the Lord," she said. "Some of these assignments present themselves as opportunities, others as difficulties. In the difficult times, we get to choose whether we will respond by drifting away from God or trusting Him and pressing in closer to Him. Right now I've got Parkinson's." The reality of that statement hung in the air. "How am I going to deal with my current assignment?"

I'm wondering the same thing about mine.

Jack interrupted my thoughts. He leaned forward and said, "You can never go back to a spiritual experience. You can remember it. You can revisit it. But you cannot relive it. What you need now, Torry, is a refreshing and renewing, and you can get *that* right where you are."

I nearly choked. I knew he was right, but this truth was going to take some time to digest. And I could start by finally admitting something to myself: My relationship with the Lord was lukewarm, and my faith had become mild.

I called Rob and told him about my conversation with Pastor Jack and Ann, and I shared honestly with him about how I was spiritually struggling. Shortly after our talk, he texted me Isaiah 43:18-19: "Forget the former things; do not dwell on the past. See, I am doing a new thing! Now it springs up; do you not perceive it? I am making a way in the wilderness and streams in the wasteland."

I appreciated the encouraging word and I knew Rob meant well by sending it, but I honestly have to say I was also a little annoyed because I didn't "perceive" that verse in my heart. I didn't see a "new thing," and I didn't see the "way" that God was making for me. Nothing was "springing up," except old feelings of self-doubt.

But here's the thing. Even when we're lukewarm, God is still calling us. Our ability to clearly hear Him depends on our spiritual proximity. When we drift away, His voice becomes less of a roar and more of a whisper. It's the type of whisper that I can only describe as—the call of the mild. And if we quiet our spirits, rid ourselves of distractions, and listen closely, we'll hear it.

The question then is...will we respond?

Revelation 3 tells us that God hates it when we're lukewarm, and I think we should hate it too. I knew I was only going through the motions in my walk with the Lord, and I hated it. I hated my mildness so much that I traveled to Alaska to get rid of it. But I discovered it wasn't my location that needed changing. It was my heart.

When I lived in Alaska, it was easy to be close to God because He was all I had. I had no career, no money, no TV, no internet, no distractions of any kind. I was fully dependent on Him for everything, and He responded in miraculous ways. Now, while it appeared that I had everything, my focus was on everything else except God. And the lack of His presence in my life led to my spiritual sleepwalking.

I knew that I wanted to move on to higher ground with God, but I wanted to be airlifted there, not to have to climb out of the valley myself. Moving on wasn't going to be simple, especially because I had dug a pretty deep hole.

I felt like the Cowardly Lion and was so afraid of failing that I lacked the courage to even make the attempt.

FLUSHED WITH SUCCESS. It took a while to locate a place suitable enough to sign my very first book contract, but I finally found it—the Incinolet toilet. Kodak captured the moment.

MY BUDDY, PASTOR JACK "BANG BANG" AIKEN. He'll lead you to the Lord one way or the other.

25

EYES WIDE OPEN

I left Alaska and had one more stop before I went home: Washington State, where I planned a three-day visit with my parents. I called Rob from the Anchorage airport to pray together, as we always did before a plane trip. (We trust God more than we do the Friendly Skies.)

"There's something else we need to pray about," Rob said. "I think I might have to take Moose in to be put to sleep."

It was an unexpected kick in the gut.

"What? No! I'll be home in three more days. Is he that bad? Can't you wait?" I begged.

"It's time, Torry. I can tell he's suffering."

We had prayed for one more year with our beloved dog, and God had answered with a yes. It was almost a year to the day since Moose had been healed, but within the last week, he had suddenly gone downhill *fast*. He couldn't stand up unaided, and he wasn't eating. Rob had even picked up some precooked game hens from Sam's Club, figuring that if anything would get Moose to eat, those would. But Moose took only a few nibbles and lost interest.

I didn't want Moose to suffer while waiting for me to return, so I asked, "Should I come straight home now?"

"No. There's nothing you can do here. You need to go see your parents."

Sadly, Rob and I agreed to have him put to sleep the next day— on Friday. And we would arrange a final Skype session for me to say goodbye to Moose that morning. I have no idea what dogs think when they see people on Skype, but I sure hope he recognized that it was me on the screen—although my diminutive size on the computer must have confused him. Not only did I appear to have lost weight, but I had also lost height.

I looked Moose in the eyes as well as I could, and I told him what a good dog he was and how blessed we were to have him as a part of our family. With tears flowing freely and my voice breaking, I told him just how much I loved him.

I had been confident that God would answer our prayers and give me a dog at the very same animal shelter where I had found Sam so many years ago. *Do I have it all wrong? What are You doing, God? I thought You were going to give me a new dog, not take one away.*

Later that afternoon, Rob called. "He's gone."

Rob couldn't string together any more words than that. The words themselves were excruciating enough for him, but to make things even harder, a torrential downpour of rain made it impossible for him to bury Moose. It wouldn't let up. So Rob opted to keep him wrapped up safely beneath the deck, protecting his friend until the weather cleared.

But it didn't clear. It got worse. The little creek that runs along two sides of our property flooded the yard and even spilled into the driveway.

· · · · · · · · ·

The same morning that Rob called to say we needed to put Moose down, he had been driving up the hill on the country road leading toward our house. This road was flanked by hundreds of acres of fields and trees on both sides. Rob spotted a black dog sitting in the grass on the side of the road, staring back at him. Curious, he slowed and turned around to investigate, but the dog immediately took off running across a field and vanished into the trees beyond.

Rob called me. "I just saw a dog." He told me about his encounter, but I wasn't really paying attention. *Why is he talking about some random dog when this is happening with Moose?*

"I think it was a black Lab," he said.

"Okay, but why are you telling me this?"

"I don't know. I just thought I should tell you."

"So now you did, and my response is to say…Whatever."

After hanging up, I immediately dismissed any thoughts about the other dog from my mind. But Rob couldn't dismiss it as easily because the dog kept reappearing.

Later in the day, he spotted the black dog on the north side of the country road several more times. The dog never crossed over to the other side. Rob would stop, get out of his van, and try to call out to the dog. But each time, the mysterious dog would take off running a quarter mile through the woods and reappear somewhere else along the road. Then Rob would see it again, and when he slowed down, off it ran. The dog fled to what it perceived as safety—into the woods.

Rob wondered if *this* was the dog I had been sensing.

The next morning, Rob was driving to work along the same country road down from the mountain, past fields and forests. Though he was still mourning Moose, his thoughts kept being invaded by this mysterious black dog. It didn't make sense. So Rob prayed, "Okay, God, if this is the dog, let me see it."

At that very moment, the black dog suddenly popped its head above the railing along the side of the road. Strange. Even stranger, the dog wasn't in its usual location; it was about a quarter mile from where Rob had seen it before. Rob got out of his van and called out, but again the dog bolted into the woods.

On Saturday, driving along the same country road leading away from our house, Rob spotted the mysterious black dog a couple more times. On one of those occasions, he saw a man putting out dog food.

So Rob pulled over and talked to the man, and he learned that the county animal control unit was planning to come out the next week and put out a trap for the dog.

Rob told me he prayed and asked God, "What do You want me to do?"

He sensed the words "Get creative."

That's when Rob landed on the idea to build his own snare. Five years earlier, he had seen an episode of the TV show *Man vs. Wild with Bear Grylls* that devoted only a three-minute segment to making snares. But Rob remembered it because he has a mind like a steel trap (which, of course, he could probably make himself). Seriously, Rob can do *anything*—except his own laundry.

On Sunday morning, Rob set about making his snare. He located a springy maple sapling that was about 12 to 15 feet long. He used a ratchet strap to attach the sapling to a tree. He then attached a snare to the top of the sapling, causing it to bend over, and he used a two-foot-by-two-foot piece of plywood to hold the snare down against the ground. The plywood served as the trigger, and when the dog stepped on it, the snare would be released. Next to the looped snare on the ground, he placed dog food to lure the stray. Then he strategically put brush on both sides of the plywood to create a funnel so if the dog wanted the food, it was going to have to walk right across the board that released the snare. NASA couldn't have built it better.

Finally, Rob placed his bright orange hunting hat on the highest point of the bent-over sapling so that it would fling off the hat when it was triggered. The snare was about 50 yards from the road, but he could still see the hat from there. If Rob drove by and saw that the hat was gone, he would know the trap had been triggered. He didn't like the thought of the dog being caught out there for hours, so he planned to check the snare every 30 minutes.

Having just arrived home from Alaska, I was unpacking my car when Rob pulled into the driveway.

"I just set a snare for the dog," he said.

"What dog?"

"The one I told you about."

"You set a snare? Who are you, Crocodile Dundee?"

"Come on, let's go check it," he said.

"Right now? But you said you just set it."

"I know," he said.

"At least let me get my luggage in the house."

Rob grabbed my suitcase and threw it in the door. "Come on."

"The kittens haven't even seen me yet."

"Let them think the world is a beautiful place for another hour."

"What's your rush?"

"I have a feeling."

"About what?" I asked.

"I think the dog'll be there."

"Why?"

"Because *you're* home."

There was something in the way he said it that I couldn't argue with. "Let's go," I said.

Heading down the country road, my thoughts were on burying Moose. I wasn't excited at all as we drove toward the trap. I was more annoyed. When you lose a dog, the idea of going through this heartbreak again in 12 to 14 years gives you pause. I needed confirmation, so I prayed out loud in the car. "Father God, if this is the dog You want for us, then let me see it too." I paused and corrected myself. "No. Let it be caught in the snare."

"Don't do that," Rob said. "You're being too prayer-specific." He knew I was hesitant about this dog and that I was purposely being specific because if the dog wasn't in the trap, I could say this wasn't the dog for us. Rob knew how seriously I took signs.

But I didn't take back my prayer. Instead, I doubled down. "Lord, if this is the dog for us, let it be caught in the snare and singing 'Freedom'—the George Michael version."

Rob slowed down as we approached the place where he had set the snare. The orange hat was gone. Rob stomped on the brakes, threw open his door, hopped out, and started walking fast. "C'mon!"

From a distance, we could hear what sounded like a faint whining coming from the woods.

"You hear that?" I said.

"Sounds like George Michael," he replied.

Feeling like I was about to be blown away, I took out my phone and began filming. And as we made our way through the trees and brush, we saw it. In the small clearing, the snare had caught the dog.

"Incredible," I said. What was even more incredible was that all of this had happened only minutes after Rob sensed the dog would be there—and only moments after I had prayed.

What do you know? I got one through the "prayer ceiling"!

As Rob released it from the snare, the dog lay on its side, as if saying, "Please, help me!" The dog looked at us like we were heroes, setting it free from the nasty snare. That's when I got my first look at this dog's face, and I was taken aback. I felt like I was looking into Sam's face.

Sam had been part black Labrador and part Airedale. This dog was part black Labrador and part huskie, giving it an Alaskan connection. The dog's head and body looked like Sam, but its curled tail was all Alaskan huskie. It also had the same soft fur as Sam.

The dog wasn't aggressive at all. Rob carried it back to the van, and we drove home with it in the backseat. I turned around and noticed for the first time that it was a female.

"It's a girl," I told Rob.

"Samantha," he answered.

"What?"

"We'll call her Samantha."

"No," I said hesitantly. "I want to think about it a little bit."

I wasn't sure if I liked the idea of giving her the female version of the name Sam. The name meant too much to me, and I wasn't going to apply it to just any old dog. Besides, I always liked wilderness names like Moose, Bear, Willow, and River—names that conjured up the natural wonder of the Last Frontier. I had Alaskan-themed pets to go with an Alaskan-themed house.

I proceeded to hunt up Alaskan huskie names online, and a whole list came up, but none of them seemed right. Then, on a whim, I put in the search words, "Definition of Samantha," and this was what I found: "Of English and Hebrew origin, most accurately means 'God heard.'"

God heard.

Those words resounded in my spirit. I was gobsmacked, as the British like to say—or perhaps I should say "God-smacked."

I pushed away from my desk and walked into the living room, where Rob was seated. "We're naming her Samantha," I said.

"I know," he responded.

While Rob "de-ticked" Samantha, I went down to see the newborn kittens for the first time since returning home.

I noticed that the black one already had his eyes open, so I held him first. The other two still had their eyes closed because it takes seven to ten days for newborn kittens to open them. But as I picked up one of the two gray kittens, I witnessed a miraculous moment. She opened her eyes for the very first time! She looked around at the world with surprise, going, "Oh my, everything is so colorful and beautiful and—"

I struck a pose, showing her my coy but approachable "head shot" face from the right. (It's my best side.)

"—oh my word, you are HUGE!"

I didn't care if she thought I was enormous. Most people think that. I just cared that mine was the very first face she saw, and it wasn't on an eight-by-ten glossy. I held this kitten for maybe three or four minutes, and then I looked at the other gray kitten. She was just starting to open her eyes too, and I realized...*my* eyes were beginning to open as well.

The spiritual fire that I sought in Alaska was starting to show sparks of life right here in my own backyard. And speaking of our own backyard, we still had a somber ceremony to perform there—burying Moose.

Rob and I started digging the hole, and Bear—Moose's best friend—left his comfortable spot on the deck and came out to be with us. I watched Bear as he lay down by the grave, right next to Moose's body, which was wrapped in his favorite blanket.

The rain may have stopped, but the tears were flowing again as we finished digging the hole. Poor Bear. Moose had essentially raised him, and now Bear wouldn't leave his friend's side. He continued to lie there by the grave until the hour became late and the shadows of evening cut across the yard. We finally had to force Bear to come back inside the house, where Rob and I comforted him and comforted each other with our favorite Moose stories.

Samantha lay near us, acclimating to her unfamiliar surroundings.

"See, I am doing a new thing! Now it springs up; do you not perceive it?"

Yes, Lord, I do.

"IT'S A GIRL!" This is our first picture with Samantha, immediately after loading her into the car.

OLD FRIENDS, NEW FRIENDS. On the left is our beloved first dog, Sam, in Alaska. The photo was taken at the head of the trail leading to our cabin. The picture of Samantha was taken in our Tennessee backyard—at the very spot where our two dogs ran off and disappeared.

26

PAWS FOR PRAYER

et's recap chapter 1 of this book.
- Missing dogs
- Heading for a conference in Cincinnati
- Hoodie pants
- DUI test
- Tap-dancing my way out of a ticket in my underwear

My journey to Cincinnati for the International Christian Visual Media (ICVM) Conference was painstakingly long, but I did take some comfort in knowing that I had so many people praying for me and my dogs. (I almost didn't even ask for prayer because I didn't want to bother people.)

Sometimes I feel like the old woman who sits in the front pew in church, and when the pastor asks for prayer requests, her hand shoots up like he just asked who wanted donuts.

"I'd like you to pray for my brother Elmer. He's got a stomach bug."

She does this every Sunday, and it seems like a different relative every time.

"My Aunt Myrtle woke up with a cough."

"My cousin Beatrice has the gout."

"My brother-in-law Walter had explosive diarrhea this morning."

First of all, how does she know so many people with names from the 1800s? Second, is she just making up these people? Is Beatrice really her imaginary friend, and if so, what kind of imagination do you have to have to give your make-believe friend gout? And third, if these are really all her relatives, either she needs to keep the entire family quarantined away from each other, or she needs to see a genetics specialist to find out what's clogging the filter of this horrific gene pool.

I know it's wrong to think this, but I feel like the prayer requests of someone like her might be glossed over a bit more than other people's petitions simply because she has so many of them. Kind of like the Boy Who Cried Wolf. Except she's the Girl Who Cried Explosive Diarrhea.

I sometimes use Facebook as my personal prayer request delivery system, figuring it's an instant way to get 5,000 people praying for me. But I also fear that people might not pray at all if I request prayer too often.

For instance, I had been hesitant to ask my Facebook friends to pray about my missing dogs because only one week before, the dogs had disappeared for four hours. That time I had asked people to pray, and the dogs returned. So if I mentioned that they had gone missing a second time, only one week later, I was afraid my Facebook friends would think I was an irresponsible pet owner. And I didn't want to annoy folks by asking for prayer again.

After searching for two days, Rob asked, "Did you post on Facebook and ask for prayer for the dogs?"

I'm like, "No. People just prayed for my dogs last week. I don't want to keep bugging them for prayer all the time."

"So you care more about your pride than you do about your dogs?"

Wrong thing to say. Those were fighting words. I was furious, especially considering that I had searched for two days with no sleep and was leaving on this trip five hours late. I shouted, "Oh yeah? Well...your...beard needs to be professionally shaped!" Again, no sleep. My comeback may have been a bit uninspired.

Eventually, however, I realized he was right. I was worried about what people would think of me, and the focus should have been on the dogs. So before I left town, I went ahead and posted: "I'm sorry to have to do this again, but my dogs are missing, and this time it's already been two days." I also explained that I was leaving for my conference five hours late and would really appreciate their prayers for safety. I soon discovered how important this minor addition to my prayer request would be.

Only 30 miles from Cincinnati, about an hour after I said good-bye to Starsky and Hutch, I found myself in yet another predicament. I wouldn't have been in trouble if my car's dashboard just knew how to talk. *If my two GPS systems can speak, why can't the dashboard learn to say something? Is that asking too much?*

But no, my dashboard just gave me this itsy-bitsy warning light in the shape of a gas pump. I never noticed it. Couldn't I have at least gotten a flashing exclamation mark? When I finally spotted the warning light, I was on empty, and there was no telling how long that little thing had been lit.

"Torry, we need to gas up...NOW!" my dashboard should've shouted at me, and maybe then it could've slapped me in the face with the gear shift. Or at least jabbed me in the side with an armrest. I'm very ticklish. I would've paid attention.

Help me make it to the next exit, I prayed. *Please, please, please!*

I expected my car to die at any second, and my eyes kept going to the gas gauge, which was now reading well below empty. I knew you get a certain number of miles after you hit empty, but who knew how many of those I had left.

Finally, I spotted an exit, and I poured on the prayers. I rejoiced as I pulled off the highway and quickly scanned the area, searching for gas stations. But I saw nothing. Who ever heard of an exit without a gas station? Did I take an exit into the Old West?

KWUFF! KWUFF!

My car began to cough like a chain smoker. No, wait. That was me.

SPUTTER! SPUTTER!

I pulled into the nearest parking lot, coasted a bit, and came to a stop directly in front of the entrance to a fitness center. The car died instantly.

Taking a deep breath and trying not to bang my head against the steering wheel, I looked over at the fitness center and locked eyes with a man sitting behind a desk. We stared at each other for about 30 seconds, and I wondered what his problem was. *Instead of just staring at me,* I thought, *maybe you can get some of those muscleheads in there to come out and carry my car to a parking spot.*

Realizing I was going to lose the staring contest, I had no choice but to get out and walk into the place, trudging through the rain. The man's eyebrows raised just a touch as he sized me up.

I stood dripping on the Welcome to Anytime Fitness rug, and I finally mustered the energy to speak. "I...have...a problem."

"I see that, and it's a big one too." (*Pause.*) "But if you sign up for a one-year membership, we can get you a personal trainer to whip you into some sort of shape in no time."

Okay buddy, first of all, not that kind of problem, I thought. *And second, what do you mean by "some sort of shape"?* A donut was some sort of shape, but I didn't think "round" was what this guy was going after.

Turning off this stream of thoughts, I sighed. "Do you have gas?" I said.

(*Another pause.*) He looked embarrassed. "Sorry. It's the protein shake."

That hit me as funny. Holding back my smile, I explained. "I meant gas for my car."

"Oh," he said. "Right."

Gassy Protein Guy gave me walking directions to the BP station, where they loaned me a gas can, and I carried a couple of gallons back, dumped it into my thirsty car, and then drove back to the station to fill up and return the can.

I finally reached Cincinnati at eight p.m., just in time to miss the entire four-hour ICVM board meeting. But I was too wiped out to worry about that. I hadn't gotten a wink of sleep the night before, and my body's tank of energy was registering empty. I wondered why God didn't put a little light in the shape of a gas pump on my forehead to indicate when *I* had run out of gas. However, I suppose drooping eyelids can serve that function. Half closed, you have half a tank of energy left. Fully closed, you're empty.

As soon as I got to the hotel in Cincinnati and apologized for missing the meeting, I decided I needed snacks. So I hopped into my car, pulled out my smartphone, and said, "Siri, where's the nearest Walmart?"

If Siri were really smart, she would've said, "Walmart? Are you crazy? You need to climb into bed and get some sleep." Instead, she obediently answered, "The nearest Walmart is 4.3 miles."

"Can you speak in a man's voice?" I asked Siri. "You sound too much like my mother."

"I can't change my voice, but you can do it yourself in Settings," she responded.

"I have *Settings*?" Sure enough, I found that you can change Siri to a man's voice, and it gave me a choice of American, British, or Australian.

I went for the American man's voice because that was as far as I could get from my mother's voice. Besides, the British guy seemed too judgmental. I figured if I asked for the nearest ice cream shop, he'd probably sigh and say, "Very well, off to the ice cream shoppe...again..."

Then I'd wonder, *What the heck is a kilometer?*

I headed to Walmart with Mr. American Siri. What could possibly happen in 4.3 miles? And for once, I was right. Nothing happened on the way there, although it did start raining as soon as I got into my car.

I arrived at Walmart in one piece, bought my snacks, and got back on the three-lane highway, heading for the hotel. The rain started coming down even harder, and the next thing I knew...

Car horns!

Sliding cars!

Skidding semis!

It was like I was in a bumper car ride, only this was real life, with cars flying every which way. I slammed on my brakes, came to a complete stop, and sat there in the middle lane in complete disbelief, still hearing the screech of tires, the crunch of metal, and the tinkle of shattering glass. I braced myself, waiting for something to crash into me, but nothing did. I seemed to be in the middle of a massive game of marbles, and a huge thumb was flicking cars into each other all around me.

As I later learned, one of the cars had put on its brakes suddenly, triggering a chain reaction in the rain. One of the semis tried to brake, and it slid sideways on the slick road. In all, seven cars and two semi-trailer trucks had been involved in the accident in front of me, but I wasn't sure how many other cars behind me might have been involved as well. All three lanes were shut down, and I was sitting in the center—the eye of the hurricane, or more fittingly, the vortex of the Torry-nado. I was completely unscathed, but I was going to be here a while.

I was stunned as I sat there looking at the chaos and watching the ambulances and police cars arrive. I was the only one who hadn't been hit by anything, and I prayed for the people around me for the next hour.

Eventually I spotted a policeman approaching me on foot, so I rolled down my window.

"How did you manage not to get hit?" he asked.

I was tempted to use my Rain Man voice and say, "I'm an excellent driver." But I caught myself and said, "I have no idea."

"Count your blessings."

I will. There's plenty of time to do that, 'cuz it looks like I may be here for three more hours.

Turns out it was only two and a half. Good thing I had snacks.

Meanwhile, the police took pictures and cars were towed away. Finally, enough of the damaged cars were moved so they could get me out of the center and maneuver another tow truck into that space. One policeman after another guided me through the maze of wrecked cars, and I had the three-lane highway entirely to myself all the way to my exit. I was very aware of God's hand of protection. The feeling was overwhelming.

· · · · · · · · ·

I believe with all my heart that the prayers from my online friends saved me on the road. If I hadn't asked for prayers, who knows where I'd have been—probably in one of the ambulances that showed up at the accident site.

We often take prayer for granted, telling people we'll pray and then forgetting to do so. But if I've learned anything about following God's calling, it's that the journey must be fueled by prayer. I have learned to appreciate a good night's sleep and a full tank of gas in my car, but prayer is even more important because that's the fuel that keeps us moving down the spiritual road.

"Be joyful in hope, patient in affliction, faithful in prayer," says Romans 12:12.

I love being joyful in hope, and I vowed to be faithful in prayer. The "patient in affliction" part must have been a typo.

Regardless, I thank my Facebook friends from the bottom of my heart. And I thank God for sending angels to my side that night.

27

THE PACK IS BACK

"They're coming!"

I didn't actually hear those two words spoken out loud. I *felt* those two words in my spirit. I know that's hard to understand, but I felt like Someone had leaned down and gently whispered, "They're coming," and I instinctively knew what it meant. The dogs were on their way home. Either that or the men with the straitjacket were coming for me. Both of these thoughts were strangely comforting. *A restful rubber room might be nice at this point.*

The ICVM board had scheduled an all-day meeting, and it was lunchtime when I was given this strong and surprising inner sense of hope. I should have been sitting at the table with my fellow ICVM board members, who were gathered for pizza, but instead I was up on my feet, pacing.

"Aren't you going to sit down with us?" asked Diane, the ICVM board president.

"No. I've got too much energy right now," I replied. *Besides, it'll sound crazy if I tell you the real reason.* "We've been sitting all morning. I just kinda want to stand...and pace."

I'd missed Friday's meeting entirely due to my string of disasters, and I inadvertently overslept this morning, showing up at nine a.m.

for an eight o'clock meeting. I felt guilty, but I hoped people understood since I'd gone an entire night without sleep the day before.

All morning I had a hard time focusing on the board meeting because the discussion was about business that didn't involve me. They were talking numbers, and numbers were my Benadryl. So like a disobedient schoolkid, I held my phone underneath the table and secretly fired off a text message to Rob. "Any word on the dogs?"

It had now been five days since they went missing.

Losing Willow was hard, but something about Samantha made her absence particularly painful to me. Over the years, all our dogs had slept in Rob's bed at night, and I always thought, *Do they like him better? Is he a better person than me? Haven't they noticed the way he crunches potato chips with his mouth open and dribbles crumbs into his beard? Oh, wait, that's it! They're in it for the easy access to snacks!*

The thoughts that our dogs preferred Rob had become the crumbs in my beard of insecurities.

Prior to getting Samantha, I'd read a dog-training book by Cesar Millan, and he pointed out that when you bring a new dog into the house, it looks for its place in the new pack. Wherever you first show the dog where to sleep, that will become its "place." Then it occurred to me: All of our other dogs had slept in Rob's bed on their first night. I didn't want them on my bed the first night because that was usually when Rob was de-ticking them. He might have missed a tick, and I'd rather it drop on his bed, not mine. So that had become the dog's place. *Yes! They don't love Rob more than me! They're probably just as annoyed by the potato chip thing as I am. The dogs are only acting on instinct!*

Following the dog whisperer's advice, I showed Samantha my room and told her to get up on the bed and lie down. I lay down with her, and she understood: This is her place in the pack. From that day on, Samantha slept in my bed. For the first time in all these years of dog ownership, I had a companion animal to keep me company at night. I was no longer alone when I woke up in the morning, and I can't tell you how good that felt. Samantha was there to greet me, nudging her head under my arm and licking my face. I thrived on it. I had a companion who met my need for acceptance and love. And the great thing about dogs is that you don't need to worry about being judged by them the way I do when I'm around people. My dogs don't care if I smoke or if I'm OCD or if I miss my writing deadline because I binge-watched *Gilmore Girls* for six hours. I mean sports. I watch six hours of sports all the time. Go...Seattle...Seagulls! Yay!

Samantha healed some of my insecurities, but she had her own fears to deal with. She'd been abused and would cower whenever she heard the word *no*—even when someone just said the word in normal conversation. She peed every time she thought she was in trouble. Kind of like me when Rob opens my credit card statements. She would also pee in excitement every time she saw me, even when I was only gone for 20 minutes. It took three weeks of affection and building up her trust for her to stop doing those things.

For me, it was the closest I could get to feeling like a parent lying next to his newborn baby every morning, looking into his child's adoring face. I had five weeks of this glorious experience, and now Samantha was gone. And it felt like God had gone deaf.

The ICVM board meeting continued on through the afternoon, and I continued to be distracted. I had a notebook in front of me, and every now and then I would write something down to pretend I was engaged. When I took out the notebook later in the meeting, I noticed I had written the number 500, the phrase "Impact It Now," and the question, "Pastry budget?"

I have no idea what any of those referred to.

Then I felt another whisper in my spirit: "They're close."

The whisper felt so strong that I immediately stood up in the middle of the meeting, and every eye turned to me. I was as surprised as they were that I was upright. I briefly debated whether to take a heroic stand on the pastry budget, but I decided instead to stay silent. I looked at my phone because something told me it would prove to be significant. It was exactly 4:07 p.m.

"Torry, we still have an hour and a half of the meeting left," said Diane.

"And I still have a bladder," I replied quickly while shoving my phone back into my pocket.

Again, I couldn't tell them what I sensed because they'd think I was nuts. And yes, I know that my statement might have been misleading and that I used it as an excuse to duck out of the meeting. But technically, it wasn't a lie because I *did* still have a bladder—and indeed, still do.

Our meeting was on the sixteenth floor, so I hopped on the elevator and rode it down to my room on the fourth floor. *Please, Lord, let our dogs be home. Please, Lord!* I didn't think I could text Rob again because I had just done it at lunch. Every time I talked to him, I could tell it was as difficult for him to say the words, "The dogs are still missing," as it was for me to hear them.

I decided I was going to call him anyway and had just reached my room when I suddenly felt the gentle vibration of my smartphone. When I pulled out the phone...boom! A photo of Willow appeared! Then, boom! Another photo came through—this one of my beloved bed buddy, Samantha!

They're home. My dogs are home!

I had a glory fit right then and there. I let out a couple of whoops and started jumping up and down while screaming, "Thank You, Father! Thank You, Father!" The poor people in the room below me probably thought an excited, overweight kid whose father had given him a one-pound Hershey bar was about to crash through their ceiling.

I quickly called Rob, and he told me he had just finished searching for the dogs and posting fliers when he was coming up the stairs of our backyard deck and looked to the right. There they were: Samantha and Willow, just coming through the trees of the forest at the end of the backyard...

At 4:07.

Something was wrong though. The dogs were moving at a snail's pace.

Rob told me how he had darted down from the deck to meet them in the yard, and when Samantha spotted him, she was overjoyed. She tore off in his direction, but then she suddenly pulled up short, looked behind at Willow, then ran back to walk with her. Willow was limping and moving slowly. Unable to control her excitement, Samantha once again bounded back toward Rob. But once again she stopped partway, turned around, looked back at Willow, and dashed back to her side.

Finally, Samantha gave Willow's face a few licks, as if saying, "Sorry, but I've just gotta do this," and charged toward Rob, this time burying herself in his arms.

To me, the fact that the two had stayed together for the entire five days was nothing short of a miracle. We'd had Willow for more than three years, and though she'd never disappeared for more than two hours before, she knew her way back home. But we'd only had Samantha for five weeks, so if they had gotten separated, she wouldn't have been able to find her way back.

Willow's leg was injured, and her entire body was covered in tiny cuts. Our place was surrounded by hundreds of acres of briar bushes, blackberry patches, and thick forests, all of which could have cut her. But some cuts were deeper. Rob thought that those were injuries from fighting animals because Willow had probably been hunting for their food for the past five days.

Willow is a mountain cur, and they are fierce. This was the kind of dog the pioneers brought with them because they will attack a bear, going straight for its face. Ever since we brought Willow to live with us, I had kept a death tally. She had killed twenty-three squirrels, eleven birds, sixteen rabbits, seven small possums, nine voles, four full-sized raccoons, and one turtle. If there had been a partridge in a pear tree, it would have been dead two years ago. Along with a whole backyard full of French hens, calling birds, and swans a-swimming. We don't talk about the twelve drummers she has trapped in our shed.

Rob took Willow to the vet, where she was given antibiotics because her leg had become infected. But just knowing my dogs were safe put me on cloud nine, and I found myself making the leap to clouds ten and eleven, telling everyone, "My dogs are home! My dogs are home!"

(Incidentally, cloud eleven is still mostly full of Cubs fans. Kinda annoying, so you may want to skip on to cloud twelve.)

.   .   .   .

I'll never know what happened to Samantha and Willow during those five days because I don't think they ever plan to publish their memoirs. But I'm pretty sure they faced obstacle after obstacle, just as I had during my travels. Despite the odds, they had persisted in their search for home, and I had persisted in my prayers and my stubborn hope that we'd get them back.

Just because you know your calling doesn't mean it's going to be a smooth path. There will be briar patches and thornbushes and fierce, full-sized raccoons trying to block you every step of your way. So you need to keep going, keep hoping, keep praying. No turning back. Persistence.

Whenever I think of the story in Luke 18 of the widow who kept coming back to the judge, begging him for justice against her adversary, I imagine my feisty Grandma Burmaster in that role. She'd be the one at the courthouse every day fighting for her right to larger parking spaces.

This judge "neither feared God nor cared what people thought," Jesus said (verse 2), and he kept refusing the widow's pleas. But she wore him down, and the judge finally decided to give her justice just so she would leave him alone.

Then Jesus said that if an unjust judge will listen to persistent pleas, think how much more God will listen. He will bring justice for His chosen ones "who cry out to him day and night."

I had cried out to God day and night for sure. I had been obsessed, and the people around me probably thought I was nuts. But love is an obsession. So be obsessed with your loved ones. Be obsessed with God. Be so obsessed with your calling that you can't keep from praying.

Then hope. Expect. Wait. The Hound of Heaven is coming.

28

A SEAT AT THE TABLE

Well, that went better than expected.

The ICVM Conference had shown the South African movie I acted in, and I was pleasantly surprised at the positive response, despite my PTSD from the experience. It wasn't perfect, but the visuals were stunning, and the message about following your calling had come through loud and clear. I was pleased.

My good day continued with the awards ceremony that evening. And afterward I walked to the German MainStrasse neighborhood, where many of the conference-goers had flocked. This area was filled with restaurants, bars, and music.

I arrived late and found the ICVM movers and shakers gathered in the outdoor section, pushing three tables together. I was looking forward to hanging out with my film friends. ICVM is one of the best conferences for networking, and not just because the people who attend are extremely talented visionaries in the Christian entertainment world. They are also some of the kindest, strongest Christians I know.

My now very good friend, Sharon Fincannon, spotted me arriving. "Torry, there's a seat at the end of the table!" she shouted while pointing at an empty chair. I couldn't believe it. At last, this was my chance. After all of my experiences of eating alone in high school, Boom-Boom had finally found a place at the cool kids' table!

Before I could reach the seat, however, someone else sat down in it. With a little vegetable oil, I probably could have squeezed in somewhere, but people appeared engaged in conversations, and I didn't want to just stand there feeling awkward, as if I were back in high school. Besides, I kinda felt something in my spirit was saying, "There's not a seat for you here," and I thought it meant I wasn't supposed to sit down. I decided to wander down the street a bit instead, figuring by the time I came back, maybe there'd be an open chair. Besides, I noticed a pet store nearby, so I thought I'd do a little window shopping for something to bring home for the dogs.

As I looked into the pet store window, I heard some Irish music coming from a bar a couple of blocks down the street. When I was in Ireland, I found the pubs to be bustling centers of food and frolicking, with people telling stories, singing, and playing pool and darts. When the people in a Dublin pub had learned I was a writer, they had gathered around me and started spinning their own yarns. Irish folks love to tell tales, and theirs were hilarious.

So, being Irish, I felt obligated to check out the place. I figured that if this pub was anything like the ones in Ireland, I'd have ten friends in a matter of minutes. However, when I passed through the doors, I found that although the bar was filled with music, it was devoid of people. There were a few folks in the far back room playing darts, but in the main room there were only two bartenders.

I took a seat at the bar, ordered an unsweetened tea, and struck up a conversation with the two bartenders—one of them a guy named Ryan and the other a girl I'll call Colleen. She was a pretty, petite woman who looked like she could be a model but cussed like a sailor. Perhaps she was a model sailor.

Ryan and Colleen were fascinated that I had recently gone to Ireland, and we chatted about the Emerald Isle a bit. But then they went to go wash some bar glasses and broke off into a conversation of their own, which I couldn't help but overhear.

Ryan said, "Has he texted you back yet?"

"No," said Colleen. "I had a friggin' abortion two days ago, but he's completely ignoring me. I don't know what his problem is. Jerk."

It was the word "abortion" that really caught my attention.

"Is there a problem with your boyfriend?" I asked without thinking.

"There's a lot of problems with me and my boyfriend. I thought I had just taken care of the biggest one." After a pause, Colleen quietly called herself a harsh expletive and then said, "I never shoulda done it."

Over the next 30 minutes, she poured out her heart. It was as if we had switched roles, and I had suddenly become the attentive bartender listening to her story. I learned that the other bartender, Ryan, was a former boyfriend who still lived with her. But the two of them also shared an apartment with her *current* boyfriend, whom I will call, let's see...since he worked at a German bar down the street, how about Adolf?

Colleen and I talked and talked until the bar closed at one a.m., so she suggested we head to the bar where Adolf worked because it was open for another hour. Ryan told Colleen he would close up, so she and I left and made our way to the German bar. But when we walked into the place, Colleen stopped in shock and stared. Adolf was locking lips with her best friend (whom I will call Eva Braun).

The next thing I knew...

Glasses flying!

Shoving!

Slapping!

Tables overturned!

Colleen hurled a shot glass at her boyfriend, but it whizzed past his head, shattering against a mirror. Someone even threw a bar stool, and it landed right next to me.

Finally, a seat!

It was high drama. But in the midst of the shouting, cursing, and airborne objects, Colleen pointed at me. "I've only known this (insert curse word) for an hour," she screamed, "and he cares more about me than all of you put together!" I was stunned, not by her calling me a curse word, but by the compliment. Colleen ran out of the bar and into the night.

I hesitated for a moment, but I knew what I had to do. I had to go after her. Just as I made for the door, Ryan walked in. He looked around at the aftermath of the bar fight as employees swept up glass, mopped the spilled drinks, and set tables back upright.

"What happened in here?" he asked.

"Colleen," I said.

He looked at me quizzically.

"Adolf was kissing her best friend," I said.

"I'm gonna go look for her."

"I'll help you."

"You go that way," he said, pointing one direction, "and I'll go this way."

So we split up, and I was only a block or two away when I heard her crying in a small alley by the pet store. I suggested we sit at a nearby table on the main drag so she could collect herself.

"No wonder he wanted me to get an abortion," she whispered.

Colleen and I wound up talking together until seven that morning. And as we talked, I was able to draw on things I had learned at the "A Time to Hope, a Time to Heal" conference—the one in which Jennifer O'Neill had shared openly about her own abortion. I had been the only male speaker at that conference, and at the time I remember thinking, *Why am I here?* But I now believe that God was preparing me for this very conversation.

Colleen asked me if I thought her pain would ever go away.

I paused and considered before I responded, "I don't think so." She gave me a stunned look as I continued, "Not on its own."

Colleen told me that the previous two nights, she had dreamed she heard a crying baby. In the dreams, she searched frantically for the baby but couldn't find it. We didn't acknowledge it, but we both knew what the dream meant.

"We've all done things that haunt us," I said. "I know I have."

I shared some of the mistakes in my own life, telling her, "In my heart, I know God has forgiven me, but I still struggle with forgiving myself."

"Do you really believe all of that (insert curse word)?" she asked.

"Yep. I believe every last word of the Bible," I told her.

"So does my grandma."

She then told me about her rough upbringing and how she and her sister had been raised by their grandmother, a loving Christian woman. It was her grandmother whom Colleen eventually called to pick her up that morning. Colleen asked if I could stay with her when she talked to her grandma, because she wanted me to be there when she told her about the abortion—a tough conversation. It was an unexpected turn for me to be involved at all.

When the grandmother arrived, she was initially irritated that she had been called out in the early hours.

"What's going on? Was he drunk again?" the grandmother asked, obviously angry that Colleen was even seeing this boyfriend.

"No...it's...uh...He cheated on me and I...I...had an..." She pointed to me. "Can you?"

Can I? Another unexpected turn, but I understood. I took the grandmother aside and carefully explained that Colleen had had an abortion two days earlier.

"What?" the grandmother said. Almost instantly, the grandmother's anger softened. She went from "You woke me up at six a.m. to pick you up at a bar" to "You should have called me at two a.m. I would've been here." Then her grandmother added, "Come back home."

The grandmother offered to help her move out, and I began wondering if I too should offer to help. But I had been given a free ticket to attend the International Christian Retail Show (ICRS), another major event in Cincinnati that overlapped with the ICVM Conference. I was anxious to attend it because of the great networking possibilities. But Colleen said, "Too bad we can't rent a truck. I've got a lot of stuff."

Without hesitation, I said, "I can help you," realizing what those words were going to cost me professionally. "The backseat of my car is empty. We could fill it up, but we can't use my trunk. It's packed for the apocalypse."

She gave me a puzzled look.

"Have your grandmother explain," I said.

* * * * * * * * *

I thought God didn't have a seat for me at the table. It turned out He did, but it was a different seat at a different table, and not one where I could pass around my business cards and promote myself. This was a seat at a deserted table on a sidewalk by an alley, with a woman who'd had an abortion. That's the chair where I was supposed to sit.

Sometimes we get so wrapped up in our careers and ministries that we miss our first and most important calling. Jesus made it clear in Matthew 22:37-40: "'Love the Lord your God with all your heart and with all your soul and with all your mind.' This is the first and greatest commandment. And the second is like it: 'Love your neighbor as yourself.' All the Law and the Prophets hang on these two commandments."

All of life hangs on these two commandments. If you don't get anything else out of this book about our calling, it's this: Our first call is to love God and love others. Everything else about our calling is subject to this. If you don't have those first two things right, none of the other things even matter.

My thoughts drifted back to my dogs. Samantha had stayed with Willow in her pain every step of the way home. Samantha wanted to race off to Rob, but she knew Willow needed her, even during those final steps to the house. Likewise, I was tempted to race off to ICRS, but I knew Colleen needed me all the way up to unloading the final box in her grandmother's house.

Racing ahead is what we do best. But sometimes I'm in such a hurry to get somewhere, all in the name of God, that I fail to see the people He has placed in my path.

Sometimes with God, what looks like an interruption is really an invitation.

29

PICK ME!

I missed the International Christian Retail Show completely. Never stepped one foot in the door. But I didn't care. My conferences were over, and I was ready to get home to my dogs. And the road trip home should be smooth sailing, right?

Have you learned *nothing* from this book?

It was a Wednesday night, and I planned to head home the next morning, but I needed a few supplies. (Okay, I'll admit...it was Metamucil because the conference food was not setting with me right.) So I drove to the nearby Dollar General store, and I had just pulled into the parking lot when I heard a horrific sound—the sound of metal slamming into something.

What now? I thought. I turned around, expecting to see that the back half of my car had fallen off.

It hadn't. Another vehicle had driven headlong into a lamppost about 15 feet away, and the post had put a deep V in the hood of that vehicle. If the post hadn't been blocking the way, that car would have driven full-speed right into me.

I made a mental note to check my Bible to find out if angels ever take the shape of lampposts.

Fortunately, the driver wasn't hurt, and the police arrived and took care of him, but by this time I was paranoid about getting into an accident. I didn't even bother going into Dollar General, Metamucil or no Metamucil. Wasn't it Winston Churchill who said, "I'd rather be constipated than dead"? No, that sounds more like me.

As I drove back to the hotel, I turned on my headlights even though it wasn't dark because I wanted to be seen. If I could have painted my car orange and mounted flashing lights, I would have.

I made it back to the hotel in one piece and went to bed early (eight p.m.). I wanted to get up at four a.m. to beat the traffic out of Cincinnati—and more importantly, to get back to my dogs.

There was only one little problem. When I arrived at the hotel at seven thirty, it was still light outside, and I accidentally left my headlights on. In the morning, my car's battery was as dead as a doornail. A security guard offered to give me a jump.

"Thanks. I was about to call AAA, which I now have on speed dial," I said. I wound up giving the security guard a copy of my book *Of Moose and Men*. I think it may have been the millionth copy I've given away.

Finally! I was on the road home. I was three hours into my drive, talking on the phone with my friend Tony Senzamici, who played the policeman in *Heaven Bound*, when...

SPUTTER! SPUTTER!

My eyes went straight to the dashboard. Evidently I was so wrapped up in my conversation that I hadn't noticed my gas light had come back on. I had (you guessed it) run out of gas—again. *I wish there was some kind of indicator on the dashboard, some kind of needle that measured how much gas was left in a car. Man, you'd think in this age of technology...*

That's when I realized where I was—back on the exact same road where I took my DUI test at McDonald's! I was now convinced that this road led straight into the Twilight Zone. In fact, I wouldn't have been surprised if Rod Serling suddenly appeared, saying, "There is a fifth dimension beyond that which is known to man. It is the middle ground between cluelessness and chaos, between wrench lights and gas lights. This is the dimension where calamity and stupidity combine. It is an area we call...the Torry Zone."

But you know what? By this time, I welcomed any interruptions. I invited God into my situation and asked Him for a gas can. Sure enough, an SUV soon pulled up behind me.

"You having vehicle problems?" the guy asked me.

"I ran out of gas again."

"And how exactly does a person run out of gas *again*?"

He looked at me like I was someone who wasn't aware of gas stations, as if I just drove and drove until the car ran out of gas and then left it there and bought a new car. To my utter amazement, the guy was carrying a can full of gas, as well as a second can containing a gas and oil mixture to go with his chain saw in the backseat. He even had a towrope. He was a regular AAA all by himself.

Not only did the guy let me use his gas, but he followed me all the way to the nearest station, about five miles down the road, just to make sure I got there. He was a saint. Saint AAA. (If you look under "Saints" in the Yellow Pages, he'll probably be the first one listed.)

So I gave him my thanks and a copy of my book, and I was on my way once again. But God had more lessons for me to learn.

About three miles from that gas station, I spotted a car stopped on the side of the road with its blinkers on. Before this week, I probably would have blown on by, anxious to get home to see my dogs. But not this time. I had learned my lesson. I needed to slow down and see if I could help. I pulled up behind the car, ready to do my Good Samaritan deed. Or, since I'd learned this lesson from my dog, my Good Samantha deed.

I noticed through the back window that a dog was sitting in the backseat. A man stepped out of the car and slowly approached me. I gulped. He had a huge machete strapped to his right hip and a very large hunting knife attached to his left hip.

I had just stopped to help Freddy Krueger.

After all of the terrible mistakes on this trip, I was afraid that stopping to help the machete murderer might be the biggest mistake of all. Overcoming my fear, I got out of my car and met him halfway.

It turned out that he was just a nice guy who liked enormous knives. He said he needed some wire to hold up his muffler, which was dragging on the ground.

"I'm sure I've got something in my trunk," I said.

When I opened the trunk, he exclaimed, "That's a whole lotta something in there."

"I'm prepared for any situation. However, I'm making a mental note right now to keep a suit of shining armor in here just in case I encounter a man with a machete." He didn't laugh at my joke but just kept staring into my trunk while I rummaged around. As it turned out, I happened to be carrying some decorative wire I had used in a Christmas show, and it was perfect for holding up his muffler.

After securing his muffler and climbing out from under his car, he brushed himself off and said, "Thanks, dude, you're a lifesaver. Is there any way I can thank you?"

Looking past him, I stared at the German shepherd in the backseat, and I meekly responded with the high, hesitant voice of a child. "Can I pet your dog?"

"Sure."

So I got into the car and gave the dog a couple of pats while I introduced myself to the woman behind the steering wheel.

"Hi, I'm Torry Martin, random dog petter. Nice to meet you. I'll only be a moment."

Petting the dog a few times gave me enough "dog energy" to get me the rest of the way home.

"Thank you," I said, but before I left, I ran back to my car to get a copy of my book for Machete Man. (Eventually I'd really like to *sell* one of those things.)

"I want a copy too," the woman said.

"You're driving. He can read his copy out loud to you."

I was now only 15 miles from home, and I am happy to report there were no more accidents or downpours or running out of gas or screws in the tire. But I did make one last pit stop, driving to the Walmart in Sparta.

(Yes, Siri, I'm going to Walmart again. But I know exactly where this one is located because it's in my hometown! So I don't need to bother you for directions, Siri, unless you just want to talk. The sordid love triangle that I'm sensing between you and Mr. and Mrs. GPS must be very difficult. I'm here for you.)

I went straight to the pet section, where I bought three different kinds of cat food and some assorted pet toys. Then I headed to the grocery section to get them milk and ham slices, and I grabbed two containers of Metamucil—one for home and one for my trunk (in case of future apocalyptic intestinal emergencies).

When I finally pulled into my driveway and crossed the threshold of my home, it was the best welcome ever. I called out their names, and Bear, Willow, and Samantha came charging toward me. It was a great celebration, filled with much jumping and licking. And the dogs got in on it too!

* * * * * * * * * *

When I was a kid on the playground in grade school, I would always have to watch as other kids were picked for kickball teams and I was left standing alone. I wasn't hopeful. I always knew I'd be last. And I could always tell that the captain of the team felt like he'd been stuck with me.

In contrast, my dogs' reaction made me feel like I was their first pick. And when God picks us, He makes it clear that He is *not* stuck with us. He picks us because He loves us and treasures us.

The last shall be first.

God picks the clumsy and the hurting and the rejected and the grieving and the persecuted. It's all there in the Beatitudes in Matthew 5:3-10.

Blessed are the poor in spirit,
  for theirs is the kingdom of heaven.
Blessed are those who mourn,
  for they will be comforted.
Blessed are the meek,
  for they will inherit the earth.
Blessed are those who hunger and thirst for righteousness,
  for they will be filled.
Blessed are the merciful,
  for they will be shown mercy.
Blessed are the pure in heart,
  for they will see God.
Blessed are the peacemakers,
  for they will be called children of God.
Blessed are those who are persecuted because of righ-
    teousness,
  for theirs is the kingdom of heaven.

I wish we could all react to God the way my dogs react to Rob and me whenever we call their names—with excitement and joy. We should be the ones shouting, "He picked me! He picked me!" when God calls our name. And be assured: God does call your name, beloved. He calls each and every one of us, individually, in our own unique way.

Maybe we don't have to literally run around in circles, jumping around like dogs. But symbolically, we should be running around in circles in our spirits. God, the Creator of the universe (making Him *slightly* more important than the playground captain), has chosen us. Doesn't that make you want to leap into the air at the thought?

I went to Alaska to try to recapture the spark that so many of us experience when we first devote our lives to the Lord. Instead, I found my fresh start here at home, and it began with Samantha. She can't replace Moose, and the pain of that loss will linger. But my eyes were opened, and as I looked out the back window and watched her romping around, I could see that God was doing a new thing in my backyard.

My fresh start is right in front of me.

I had thought that it was up to me to get God's attention, not realizing that He was there the entire time. It was like I thought the only way I could get God to notice me was to stand on a mountain in Alaska and scream at the top of my lungs.

"Pick me! Pick me!" I called to God, waving my arms like a crazy man.

Then He sat beside me and calmly whispered, "I already did. Weren't you listening?"

(Photo by Lucas Wilson)

30

BONUS CHAPTER!
THIRTY FOR THE PRICE OF 29!

I finished writing this book and realized that somehow, after all the editing, I came in 3,000 words *under* my word count limit. *That's a first!* Like rollover minutes, I asked my editor if I that meant I could have 3,000 more for my next book. My editor said no if I was talking about words, and "Get your Grandma's toothpicks no" if I was talking about money.

So now I have 3,000 free words burning a hole in my vocabulary. I could use them to tell a story right down to every last excruciatingly painful detail if I wanted. Three thousand is a lot of words to just waste. And the way I figure it, that's like free cable. As long as you have it, you use it. So here it is, a bonus chapter. Think of it like you would an unexpected fry you find at the bottom of the bag—as a gift.

Disclaimer: This chapter will have no point. It will not make you think. It will not make you a better person. But remember, it *is* a freebie. Like going into a dollar movie theater, you can't go to the manager and complain about the sound. You paid a dollar. So here we go.

* * * * * * * * *

Rob and I returned to Alaska for a vacation—the first time we had been there together in 20 years. My earlier trip without him had been a bit of a bummer, but now I had a freshly sheared attitude and a brand-new outlook, and I was confident that going back to Alaska together would be more fun.

One of our first stops was Golden Donuts, which has the greatest donuts in the entire state of Alaska. I was craving a warm maple bar topped with a big slab of crispy bacon. It's kind of a fad donut that has caught on quickly with some of the better bakeries, and I knew that if Golden Donuts had a bacon maple bar, it was probably the best of all time.

As soon as I walked in the door, there it was. A tray of fresh, beautiful maple bars covered with bacon and sitting on the top shelf in the very center of the donut display. I peered down through the glass to ogle them, but something was wrong. The bacon looked a little off to me. It was too perfectly flat, like someone ran over it with a steamroller.

"Is that real bacon?" I asked the lady behind the counter. She sighed, rolling her eyes like she'd been asked that question a million times. "It's turkey bacon," she told me.

Turkey bacon? Why not just use tofu and be done with it? It seemed so ridiculous that I couldn't help laughing. "Why don't you use real bacon?"

That's when the lady gave me "the look"—a frosty, stone-cold stare displaying the icicle eyes of pure judgment. "Because pork is bad for you."

"Everything in this shop is bad for me!" I burst out laughing.

Rob turned to me and joined in. "Do you really think anyone comes here for the health benefits?"

"I know, right?" I said. "Like someone's saying, 'Let's go to Golden Donuts 'cuz their donuts are healthier. They don't use pork products!'" It took me a couple of seconds of laughing to realize the lady wasn't laughing with us, and her icicle eyes were now full-blown glaciers.

With a scowl, she stuffed our two giant apple fritters into a paper bag with such force and speed that I'm surprised she didn't tear right through it. *She's probably in a bad mood due to her pork deficiency.*

She rang us up and then handed me the change and my coffee. "Did you want creamer?" she asked.

"No, thanks."

She then looked me dead in the eyes and purposefully tossed two miniature creamers straight into the bag with our apple fritters. "Just in case you change your mind," she said with a snarky-sweet tone and a villainous smile that would rival the Joker's.

We left Golden Donuts and were back on the road to the cabin, but I was more than a little annoyed. "Did you hear her tone with me?" I said. "She asked if I wanted the creamers, and I very clearly said no, but then she forced them on me anyway!" Rob opened the donut bag while I continued ranting. "I feel like my right to black coffee was intentionally violated."

Rob handed me one of the giant apple fritters.

"Are there any napkins?" I asked.

Rob looked in the bag. "Nope. She didn't give us any."

"What?"

"She didn't give us any napkins."

"Are you kidding me? That was intentional! She purposefully withheld napkins as some sort of sick and twisted act of revenge to punish us for our pork preference."

Rob looked at me like I was crazy. "Or she just forgot the napkins."

"No. She purposefully left out the napkins and threw the creamers into the bag instead. It was a passive-aggressive act of violence."

We left and headed up to see the old cabin.

I drove maybe a little too fast down the bumpy road. Rob scolded me a couple of times, but I didn't care. I was too excited. I had to slow down anyway because I had just reached the spot where our road ended at a T with another road.

I noticed a big construction bin ahead where somebody was obviously remodeling a cabin. Some of the workers had tossed a bag of their own trash onto the pile of construction trash, and five dogs were ripping into it. The bag was torn open, and there were donut boxes, pizza boxes, hamburger wrappers, and assorted Kentucky Fried Chicken containers all over the ground.

"Someone wasn't thinking. That's gonna draw bears," Rob said.

"Epic forest-life fail," I agreed while turning left at the T and watching the two huskies, one black Lab, one German shepherd, and a pretty good-sized Tibetan mastiff continue to tear the trash apart.

The 200-yard driveway just ahead took us to the trail leading to the cabin. The first thing Rob noticed after reaching the cabin were the three huge satellite dishes attached to the roof. "I'm surprised the weight of those things doesn't tip the cabin over."

I took a selfie of us in front of the dishes, and I could tell by Rob's expression that it was taking everything in him not to break out his tool set and dismantle them.

Rob had forgotten the cabin key in the hotel room, but fortunately he keeps a lock-picking kit in his wallet. (Apparently, that's where he packs for the apocalypse.) I scanned the deck while he picked the lock. My old bedroom dresser had been dragged outside, and all the drawers were filled with junk. I dug through it, and that's when I found the greatest treasure I could imagine—the Hot Stuff pepper spray I accidentally used on myself instead of an angry bear in front of our cabin. (See *Of Moose and Men* for details.) I had placed it in the back of the dresser drawer after spraying myself because I didn't want it anywhere near me in the kitchen. And there it had sat for 20 years. I couldn't have been more excited because I figured I could take this back with me to Tennessee as a souvenir!

"You can't take that in your carry-on," Rob said. "It's a weapon, so you'll have to put it in the luggage you check in. But even then, it's an aerosol, so they still might not allow it unless it's empty. You'll need to spray it all out."

Rob had successfully picked the lock, so we walked in. I could tell he was as disappointed with the inside of the cabin as he was with the satellite dishes. Everything had fallen into disrepair.

I took pictures to document our experience and even made a short video to put on the website for this book. After we finished looking at everything, we left the cabin and headed down the trail. But Rob had forgotten to lock the door, so he went back to do that.

When I reached the car, I decided to make use of the time to empty the pepper spray aerosol on the ground. I pressed the button, and a straight and steady stream of thickish, rusty fluid shot out. Some of it drizzled and trickled down the side of the can, getting on my hand. Though the pepper spray had obviously devolved into a rusty, oozing liquid over the last 20 years, the potency had not diminished. It stung!

I dropped the can on the ground and reached into the Golden Donuts bag for napkins, but of course, there were none. *That wretched, wicked donut lady!* So I wiped my hand on the bag and wiped off the pepper spray can as well. My hand still stung, so I stepped away from the car and used the last of my coffee to wash off any remaining pepper spray. Then I wiped the coffee off my hand and threw the bag into the backseat.

Meanwhile, Rob had returned. He had removed his jacket and holster to place in the backseat. When he saw the Golden Donuts bag lying in the center of the seat, he grabbed it, wadded it up with both hands, and tossed it out of his way.

Soon, he noticed his hands were burning

"Was there something on that bag?" he asked. "I crumpled it up, and now my hands are burning."

As I explained why his hands stung, we searched around for something for him to wipe his hands on. My eyes went immediately to the two miniature individual coffee creamers from the donut place. "Here. There's milk in these—it'll help the sting."

Rob poured coffee creamer all over his hands and dribbled some on his jeans, creating a mess.

"Oh," I said, reaching into the backseat. I've got a roll of paper towels in the blue travel bag."

"You have paper towels?"

"Yeah."

"Why didn't you tell me you had paper towels instead of us using a donut bag as a napkin?"

"I don't know. I guess I didn't think of it 'cuz I was so annoyed with the donut lady over the creamer incident."

"Which bag are the paper towels in?" he asked.

"The big blue one. Right next to the bottled water."

"You have bottled water?"

"Yeah."

"Why didn't you offer a bottled water to me instead making me use creamers to wash my hands?"

"Again with the accusations? Seriously? Why do I do *anything*, Rob? And why do *you* always act like I'm secretly conspiring against you and plotting your destruction?"

This went on for a few minutes and ended with Rob rinsing his hands with the bottled water and drying them with the paper towels before finally exhaling his patented "Torry sigh" and climbing into the passenger seat.

So dramatic. Big deal. The pepper spray stuff burned my hand too, but you don't see me being a big baby about it. Although it does burn, and I do want my mama.

I opened the driver's door and got behind the steering wheel. There was plenty of room to turn the car around and drive forward, but the thing is, it's a straight, 200-yard-long, dirt driveway in the middle of the wilderness. And the rental car has this cool back-up camera! When else will I have an opportunity to use it for 200 yards?

"Put your seat belt on," I told Rob. "I want to use the back-up camera."

"Why?"

"It's fun. I wish my car had a back-up camera. It's like free cable—as long as you have it, you use it. Plus it makes me feel like I'm in *Top Gun!*" I started the car. "Like I'm Maverick and you're Goose, and this is the cockpit of our F-14 Tomcat."

"I think you've got that backward. *I'm* Maverick. *You're* Goose," Rob said.

"Isn't Goose the one that dies?"

"Yes."

"No. I got it right."

Grabbing my iPhone, I went to YouTube to hunt up Kenny Loggins's "Danger Zone" music video from *Top Gun*. Then I set my phone in the spare change tray and pressed Play. The instrumental music began.

Man! No aviator glasses! I'll have to make do with my Batman Ray-Bans instead. I grabbed the sunglasses from above the visor and skillfully slid them on just as the singing began. I looked at Rob and sang with it.

"Revvin' up your engine, listen to her howlin' roar."

Rob didn't react. So I continued.

"Metal under tension, beggin' you to touch and go."

Still nothing. *Fine. Don't play along. But I'm gonna do this thing and look cool doing it. I'm already mentally committed. Committed to being cooool.* I put the car into reverse and started backing down the long driveway.

"Highway to the danger zone. I'll take you ridin' into the danger zone."

I could see in my peripheral vision that Rob was still staring at me, but I couldn't really read his expression. *He's either amazed or mystified. They're so similar that I have trouble distinguishing. I'll just assume he's impressed with my excellent backward-driving ability.*

I raised my left eyebrow as if to say, "*I know. I'm good, right?*" And just as my eyebrow had risen to its cockiest height, the back tire on the passenger side hit the far right edge of the dirt driveway and nearly pulled us into the ditch.

"Torry!" Rob yelled. I quickly corrected the car and guided it back to the center of the driveway. He looked at me accusingly after recovering from a momentary panic. "Yep," he said with a sigh. "I'm Goose."

Whatever. Don't respond to him. There's still nine or ten seconds of this awesome guitar solo to continue my coolness.

"And you're Maverick trying to kill me," Rob added.

Let it go.

"Just like he did to Goose in the movie."

Okay, that's it! I slammed on the brakes. I reached for my iPhone and shut the music video off. "First of all, you have completely ruined the 27-second Dann Huff guitar solo, and no one should ever do that. You treat that solo with respect. With reverence. Second, and most importantly, Maverick didn't kill Goose. Iceman did."

Rob responded, "Actually, it was hitting the aircraft canopy head-first after ejecting that killed him. The accident itself though? That was all Maverick's fault."

"Are you kidding me? It was Iceman's pride that wouldn't allow Maverick to get the shot at Jester. That's why he ended up in the jet wash that killed Goose."

This was just the beginning of a full five-minute discussion about who was responsible for Goose's death—Maverick or Iceman. Finally, Rob said, "In the end, it doesn't matter whose fault it is. We all knew Goose was gonna die the minute his wife showed up at Miramar in that airport scene."

Good point. That settled it. Time to move on. But he had completely ruined my coolness vibe. So I had to start over. I pulled the car all the way back up to the top of the driveway, grabbed my phone, and cued the "Danger Zone" music video back up on YouTube. "We're starting this again from the very beginning. Don't ruin the guitar solo this time."

I took off my glasses, placed them back above the visor, and then waited a second before I pressed Play. The music intro started, and I took my glasses back down and once again placed them over my eyes right at the end of the musical intro. *I look even cooler than the first time!* I turned to Rob.

"Revvin' up your engine, listen to her howlin' roar."

The problem with wearing dark sunglasses while watching a dark back-up camera screen is—well, ya can't really see. But driving to "Danger Zone" without sunglasses isn't cool, so...you suffer. For cool's sake.

Because I couldn't make out the camera screen very well, I backed up at a snail's pace while sneaking peeks over my sunglasses occasionally, all while the music was blaring.

After I had backed down the 200-yard driveway, the song still had a minute and a half to go. I could see that the main road was completely deserted, so I decided to keep driving with the back-up camera until I got to the construction dumpster. That way I could stop exactly when the song ended, pull down my sunglasses, and say...I don't know, something Tom Cruise would say. I'd figure it out on the spot.

Continuing in reverse down the main road, I looked in the back-up screen and saw that a dog was still by the dumpster, so I slowed down a little and squinted. I thought it was one of the huskies at first, but as I got closer, it looked much bigger and more like the mastiff. The dog stood on his back legs, trying to paw some food out of the trash from the construction bin. I continued to back up.

"He really is a big dog," I said.

Rob looked down at the back-up camera to see what I was talking about. Suddenly he spun his entire body around and looked through the back window.

"Bear!" Rob bellowed.

I slammed on the brakes in a panic. "Where?"

"The dog isn't a dog. It's a bear!"

I looked at Rob and then past his shoulder at the grizzly bear that was about 30 feet behind us and standing by the dumpster.

"Go!" Rob ordered as he reached for his gun in the backseat, only to be restrained by the seat belt.

He quickly unclipped the seat belt and threw it off to reach for the gun again. "GO!"

I floored it, forgetting that I was still in reverse. Rob's body slammed against the dashboard. We were now actually *closer* to the bear and had almost passed it. The grizzly was six or seven feet away from Rob's passenger window.

"What are you doing?" Rob squealed in the highest-pitched voice I've ever heard him use. Noticing that the grizzly was almost perfectly lined up with Rob through the window, I thought, *It's now or never.* I grabbed my iPhone to get a picture of Rob and the grizzly. I mean seriously, how often do you get a chance at a shot like that?

Rob was still reaching for his gun in the backseat and bumped me with his shoulder when he turned around, knocking my phone to the floorboard. It was still blaring "Danger Zone."

"GOOOOOOOOO!" he bellowed.

What happened next is what Rob now refers to as the "Herky-Jerk Retreat."

The bear was on Rob's side of the car, but the car was cockeyed on the road, so I had to quickly pull forward a few feet to straighten out. Then I slammed on the brakes, once again causing Rob to hit the dashboard with his backside.

Hypnotized by the back-up camera, I put the car in reverse and backed up a few feet before slamming on the brakes and sending Rob sailing toward the backseat. I never once looked out the front windshield. I have trained my ADHD self to focus on only one thing at a time whenever I'm experiencing sensory overload so I don't get overwhelmed. And in this instance, the one thing I chose to hyper-focus on was the back-up camera.

"Highway to the danger zone..."

I drove forward a few feet and slammed the brakes, hurling Rob into the dashboard, then slammed the car into reverse. "What are you doing?" Rob yelled.

"Ride into the danger zoooo-oooo-oooo-oooone..."

I backed up another few feet and then slammed on the brakes, slamming Rob into the backseat, and slammed the car into forward. "I don't know!" I shouted.

Again: slamming brakes, slamming Rob, slamming forward. "I'm trying!" I yelled in a panic while Rob continued to reach for the gun.

I jerked the car backward, knocking Rob's head into the visor, and I proceeded to complete what Rob now calls a 13-point half-Martin. I had somehow managed to lurch and turn the car in a complete half circle. Now, instead of the bear being almost behind the car, he was directly in front of it.

"Torry, stop!" Rob yelled at the top of his lungs. I slammed on the brakes, slammed Rob into the dashboard, and jolted to a stop. "You hit the bear!"

"No, I didn't," I replied.

Suddenly, the grizzly rose up on its hind legs, put one front paw on the trash bin to support himself, and stared directly at us. It stood completely upright.

"Ride into the danger zooooone..."

The bear was only upright for about two seconds, but time stopped as we held our breath in anxious anticipation. The grizzly looked at us through the car windshield and decided we were too stupid to bother with, I guess. He just dropped back down on all fours and ran into the woods.

Rob, breathing heavily, turned to stare at me.

"That was *so* not Maverick," I said, while looking at him and exhaling.

"What kind of driving was *that*?" Rob said. "You can't move *forward* if you're looking *backward*!"

Hmm. That's a good quote. It's kind of what this whole book is about. I should put that in there.

"What were you thinking?" he asked.

I took off the sunglasses and put them back on the visor. "I was thinking that was a good quote. Following your calling requires you to keep looking forward."

"No, what were you thinking, driving like that?"

"I don't know...there was yelling and a bear and my phone fell...there was a lot going on."

"Oh, brother!" he said.

"Didja get a picture?" I asked him.

"Of what?"

"The bear!"

"No, I was kinda busy getting a car concussion. Why didn't you take a picture?" he asked.

"I tried! But you knocked the phone out of my hands."

Rob ignored me and started checking his pockets and the backseat for something.

"I think I forgot my phone in the cabin," he said. "We have to go back."

I looked in the rearview mirror at the main road and the 200 yards of driveway stretching straight up to the cabin. I picked my iPhone up off the floorboard and cued up "Danger Zone" again. Then I pressed Play, grabbed my glasses from the sun visor, slid them on, and put the car in reverse, ready to use my back-up camera again. I turned to Rob.

"Revvin' up your engine, listen to her howlin' roar."

Rob shook his head. "Unbelievable," I heard him mutter under his breath.

I raised my left eyebrow. "I know. I'm good, right?"

For videos, photos, and more bonus chapters, check out my website: www.torrymartin.com.

DISCONNECTED. "I'm surprised the weight of those things doesn't tip the cabin over."

REUNITED. After 20 years, I'm back together again with the pepper spray from the bear encounter in *Of Moose and Men*, chapter 16, "The Flavor of Stupid."

DANGER ZONE. Goose and Maverick pose with their F-14 Tomcat just before taking off and using the back-up camera on the long runway behind them.

BEAR WITH US! Since Rob knocked my iPhone camera on the floor of the car, we had to settle for this dramatic photo reenactment of the bear encounter in which we barely survived. Only my excellent driving skills saved us.